THE TURNAROUND: 180 DAYS OF CHANGE

By Dr. Gemar Mills

TABLE OF CONTENTS

PROLOGUE

PROLOGUE

I got hired as principal of a comprehensive high school named Malcolm X Shabazz on August 31, 2011, only a week before school began. Being the fourth principal in four years, I knew that 180 days was all I had to turn the school around. This book tells the story of the 180-degree turnaround I needed in life, which prepared me for those 180 days at Shabazz. This book provides explicit strategies on how my team and I transformed the school.

Everything you will read in this book comes from my obsession with learning and doing anything I could to ensure that our youth were afforded the opportunity to receive a high-quality education despite the chaos and adversity they faced in their daily lives.

With the knowledge contained in these pages, coupled with a "By any means necessary" mindset, anyone can be the transformational leader they aspire to be. Take a journey with me as I revisit my first school year as a high school principal.

- Review documents I created and used to turn around the school.

- Learn how to structure a building for students and staff members to function efficiently.

- Understand how to create and implement a professional development plan that guarantees success.

- Discover the power of decision-making.

- Recognize and choose the data that matters and guarantees student success.

- Learn the secret to changing a school's culture.

School districts are looking for transformational leaders, not leaders who have transferred from one school to the next. All children deserve to experience a school where the culture is stronger than any social group outside its walls.

Between my determination to ensure student success and the fact that my team and I accomplished something as significant as the Shabazz turnaround, I felt it was important to share the things that worked, with any educator interested. There is no excuse for poor instruction.

PART ONE
BLACK

1 GRADUATION DAY

GRADUATION DAY

No more significant star has ever appeared on the stage at Newark Symphony Hall. He approached slowly on his crutches, step by step, to receive his diploma. With 180 of his classmates, Shea Mclean became a graduate of Malcolm X Shabazz High School in Newark, N.J.

Seeing Shea take that triumphant walk brought tears to my eyes because I know what he's overcome. I replayed in my mind the day he was in my office, describing to me how he was gunned down with an assault rifle, an AK-47. Shea told of watching his friend get shot 13 times and being unable to turn his head away from the sight. As the shooter turned back to him, Shea just closed his eyes as if he were dead to avoid getting shot anymore.

This trauma took place only seven weeks before graduation. Shea's mother, Ms. Mclean, who was a teacher's aide at Shabazz, dedicated herself to getting him everything he needed to graduate. Thanks to her, the necessary classwork, homework, and makeup material found its way to Shea's hospital bed, ensuring that he had every opportunity to complete the required tasks. Of course, just because his mom brought the materials didn't mean that Shea would do the work. Nonetheless, he did, securing his spot in Malcolm X Shabazz high school history as a class of 2015 graduate.

Just weeks after nearly being killed, Shea appeared in my office. For him just to get there was amazing. I was in awe of his courage and strength. What I remember Shea saying over and over during that visit was, "I'm done. I'm changed. I'm different. I'm never going to do that again. I'm not going to live a life like that again." He was denouncing the street life that he had once embraced. Shea was no longer interested in building a reputation in his neighborhood that instilled fear in the community.

I asked Shea if the police caught the people who shot him because he would know. He replied, "I know who shot me. I just don't want to get involved and keep it going." The rumor circulating among the students was after shooting Shea and two other people, the killers drove off in a truck, set it on fire, and blew it up behind John F. Kennedy, a neighborhood community recreation center for children. The story appeared in online news source nj.com under the headline "1 dead after the triple shooting outside Newark Police Department."

My name is Gemar Mills, and I attended graduation as the school's principal. What a journey it has been for the students, the school, and me. I come from the Christopher Columbus projects in Paterson, N.J., a place you don't visit unless you live there. I grew up amid gunfire, drugs, fistfights, gangs, and hopelessness. So have many of my students. My life mission is to protect them from those things because experiencing life like that typically leads to death or prison at a young age. Early death is a reality in the neighborhood I was raised in like many of the communities surrounding Malcolm X Shabazz high school. However, that darkness was swept away that day at Newark Symphony Hall. In its place were smiles, achievement, and hope. Girls in gold and boys in black joined to sing, "Lift Every Voice and Sing" with the lyrics:

"Facing the rising sun of our new day begun,
Let us march on till victory is won."

John Gibbons, the U.S. Marshall of the District of Massachusetts and Shabazz alum, gave the commencement address.

"Graduates," he said. "This is just the beginning of a promising road ahead. Every graduate of this 2015 class has the potential to do great things."

Valedictorian Elmy Antonio, whose achievements as a

student-athlete helped change the culture at Shabazz, also emphasized possibilities in his speech.

"When an opportunity is given to you, there's no reason to hesitate," Elmy declared. We should take that opportunity and make things happen for ourselves."

Triumph and hope were in the air, and not just for the students. Shabazz itself can take a bow on this occasion. Not long ago, amid dismal statistics and episodes such as students pelting state monitors with snowballs during a fire evacuation drill (which the students themselves caused), the state threw in the towel and recommended Shabazz close down.

In many ways, their recommendation was justified. Few people, probably not state monitors, could look at the Shabazz landscape back then and find much hope. Statistics in the accompanying chart, titled "Where We Were," tell only part of the story. The unseen part, the one that is impossible to measure, is the level of discouragement that prevailed for too long.

A documentary account by the *Star-Ledger*, New Jersey's most prominent newspaper, addressed the climate inside the building.

"In the hallways, students would fight — they'd smoke pot in the stairwells. Teachers lived in fear. When they weren't getting abused, they got ignored. Many skipped school altogether. There were no fires, but the fire alarm would go off almost daily."

Then came the Turnaround. Shabazz went from near-anarchy to a functioning school that let children learn and pursue excellence.

The Graduation Day of 2015 was a testament to it. Each student brought a story. Not all of them were as dramatic as Shea McClean's, but his struggle to walk across the stage can easily be a metaphor for what my students and the school endured and had overcome. As a community, we lived up to our school nickname — the Bulldogs. We would not give up!

I was 27 when I became principal of Shabazz. That's pretty young for such an important job, but I was wise enough to know the stakes. I was the fourth principal in four years. My mentors told me, "You're going to ruin your career." There was even a side of me that wondered if I were only getting hired until the district assembled a plan of action to shut down the school. It became evident to me that if I were to turn things around, I'd have to do it quickly. The culture would have to change in a hurry. I'd have to present my beliefs and principles to the faculty, and at some point, they would need to buy in, if this was going to work. After officially becoming the principal, knowing that the state was observing, and my belief that the district had a hidden agenda I adopted the Under Armour commercial slogan, "We must protect this house!" Thankfully, staff and students did just that.

As the students filed across the stage, I thought of my mom, who believed there was a way out of the projects and understood that education was it. I thought of other influences in my life, of narrow escapes, and of books and authors that made an impact on me. Books such as *Mindset* by Carol Dweck *Making Hope Happen* by Shane Lopez, *Reframing Organizations* by Lee G Bolman and Terrence Deal, *Grit: The Study of Passion and Perseverance* by Angela Duckworth, *Blink* by Malcolm Gladwell, and *6 Secrets of Change* by Michael Fullan. Most importantly, I thought of my colleagues at Shabazz, the people who bought into the idea that better things were possible. Those people made the pursuit of change a part of what they thought, a part of what they did, and a part of who they were.

I thought about pieces of my life — the extreme poverty and violence in my childhood, the physics teacher who showed me that commitment could bring results, and football, a sport that inspired my success and the 180-day Turnaround at Shabazz. Finally, I reflected on educational practices, which I call levers. Those are the practices that worked for Shabazz, and that can work in other schools as well. All these vivid memories ran through my mind while I watched the parade of black and gold go pass. There was hugging. Parents smile with pride and happiness. Teachers looked on, knowing they had contributed.

My purpose in education is much more profound than Shabazz—it's for all schools throughout the country that have faced difficulty with ensuring young people have the opportunity to create their success. For decades, educators have searched for the cure of student failure within school districts. Despite the many antidotes prescribed by some of education's best and brightest scholars, the problems remain and in many cases have become worse. The southward of Newark, like other areas of the city, is not the most relaxed place to grow up. Boarded-up homes, empty lots, and gangs are a part of the daily landscape.

That's the situation I stepped into; I got hired as principal of Shabazz on August 31, 2011, and school began on September 6. Thanks to my mother's guidance and the values she instilled in me, help from beautiful educators, great ideas from gifted authors, and a gut that told me what to do, the Turnaround happened. The proof is in the graduation scene unfolding in front of me and the graduates that came before it, that was filled with student success stories and me.

Nevertheless, turnarounds don't just happen. Taking over at Shabazz with very little room for error, I had to identify the mission, implement strategies, and work at them every day. It was a challenge. But we had ideas, and we took a chance.

2 IN MY PROJECTS

IN MY PROJECTS

If we ever get a chance to meet in person, you're going to see a scar on my face. It begins on my forehead, curls around my right eye, and continues down my cheek. There's a story that goes with that. On July 3, 1996, I was invited to attend a party at "The Dream" nightclub in Paterson by some of the older men in my housing projects. I was 15 at the time, which was fairly normal. Many of my friends had attended in the past, and so had I. It was never a hassle to get in. The older men from my housing projects knew security well. The night was amazing; I was like a kid in a candy store... dancing with females who were older than me. Everybody was showing me a lot of love and praise me for being a kid in this space with these older men who were showing me a good time. This group of men walked in, and the men who brought me to the club were upset. I didn't know what the tension was between the two, whether they had come from a different neighborhood or something had transpired amongst them as friends. But it wasn't good. As the night began to wind down, and the group that had come in began to leave, my friends began to leave as well. As we met up at the door, one guy of my group punched one guy from the other group in the face. Then other men from my group begin hitting him. His friends didn't do much. The guy was able to run, and my group chased him toward the parking lot. And I of course ran with the men I was with because I didn't want to be stuck back with the guys whose friend was being assaulted and have them do something to me. When I caught up with my group, they had captured the guy whom they'd punched in the face. He was trying to get into his car, and they resumed beating him. They put his head through the window. It was a champagne-colored Lexus, a GS-300. His head was all busted. His face was cut up. They kept beating on him until he couldn't move anymore. I witnessed the whole thing. I thought they had killed that man. When we left the scene, I knew nothing more than that guy was dead and we were going to hear about it on the news. We ran out of there, got back into the cars and we headed back to our projects. For me, being that age (15), I thought, "Well, okay, those aren't my everyday friends. I don't hang out with them normally. That's it. It's done, over with." But that wasn't the case.

A few weekends later, my age group of friends went

walking around the neighborhood outside of our projects. That was something we would do. The plan was to go to a party that was on the other side of town. We were underage, but we were going on the assumption that they would let us in as they have in the past. On our way there, we walked through a neighborhood we knew we shouldn't be walking through, looking for trouble. We went to a store, and on the way back, we were walking, I believe five people were ahead, and one of the guys in my group got punched in the face. My guy began running. We had one older man with us; he started running. We all began running because we weren't sure if he had a weapon of some kind. I thought that I was smart by slowing up and heading into a nearby White Castle because there was a cop in there. I never made it that far.

That's when the assault began. Unbeknownst to me, those were the guys who had come into a club a few weeks before. They remembered me. And they thought that we were of age. By the time it was over, it had taken 400 stitches to put me back together.

Such was life in the Christopher Columbus Projects in Paterson, N.J. Violence and dysfunction were everywhere. Things that would seem crazy to an outsider were the norm in my neighborhood. There were gangs, weapons, fights, and, yes, deaths.

You may ask if there was a moment where I realized I lived in a less-than-ideal environment. Here's the answer: There were a ton of moments. I remember being a kid sitting in the living room and watching TV. I was about seven or eight. Now here comes a knock on the door. Outside was Danielle, our next-door neighbor. She had about six children, and there were rumors that she was addicted to crack cocaine. I couldn't imagine what she was doing at our door because we didn't have much.

It turns out she had a reason. In my home, my family smoked a lot of cigarettes. My grandmother smoked. So did my mom, my grandfather, and my uncles. They would smoke cigarettes and dud them out in the ashtray. I opened the door for Danielle, and she came in — remember, I'm seven or eight years old at the time. She didn't say anything but went to the ashtray and began taking the cigarette butts because my family wouldn't always smoke them to the end. They would just smash them down, and Danielle came to pick them out.

My mother heard something and came into the room screaming, "Get your behind out of my house! What the hell are you doing?" At the time as a kid, I didn't understand what was going on, but I knew it wasn't normal. My mother knew it wasn't normal. Danielle was recycling cigarettes from families that lived on the floor because she couldn't afford them.

Things were not the idyllic home that you would see on a 1950s sitcom. It was the projects, located in one of the most terrible sections of Paterson, N.J. In most neighborhoods, you don't see 10-year-old children out after 8 PM without an adult. It happened all the time where we lived; we were going to T.J's, where there was a pool table, pinball machine, video games like "Streetfighter." And they had all these penny candies. So we'd be out at 1 o'clock in the morning, which is not normal, right? But it was normal for us.

I came close to being a statistic. There were plenty of statistics, and not many were good. According to New Jersey's Uniform Crime Report, in 1993, there were 2,184 reported violent crimes in Paterson, 23 homicides, 1,089 robberies and 994 aggravated assaults.

Alongside the crime was the poverty. We just didn't have anything. We were in Section 8 Housing. Our family, in this case, my mom, didn't have the means to pay rent for a three-bedroom apartment. The state's Section 8 Housing program would pay a portion of the rent to the landlord, and we would have to come up with maybe three or four hundred dollars of the bill. Sometimes less—it all depended on your household income.

People went to jail. I would say that 80 percent of the people who were arrested and then came home spent a few months trying to live their lives like law-abiding citizens. However, a few months in the project environment and the difficulty of getting employed, they would give in almost immediately—Embracing the things they were most successful at, illegal activities, all over again. They would justify why they were doing it and had no remorse. It was like, "I just need to make as much money as I can so that when I do go to jail or get killed, my family will be fine." That was the mindset where I lived.

You may be wondering why I was able to escape the projects when others never do. It's the old question of nature versus nurture. What matters more, a person's environment or a person's innate wiring? I haven't figured that out. A lot of the things you can't explain. You put it in the realm of God, who controls and navigates your life. You except there are things you can't control and live your life the best way you know how.

Tons of people live these experiences and can tell many of the stories that I know because I wasn't experiencing this alone. I'm just thankful, between my mom and the respect I have for her, she put all her love and energy into me no matter what was going on in her life. She sacrificed so I could have. I didn't need to sell any drugs because she would go without so I could have the newest pair of Nikes. That's what I needed to feel accepted amongst my peers. I respected her for that, and I just wanted to give her everything she was looking for from me.

Yes, life in the projects was tough. But it prepared me for a life in schools. I know what the kids are going through they're scared by their circumstances. Maybe they don't carry those scars on their face like I do, but you can bet that they exist. They're deep, and they're lasting. No matter how ugly they are, you can't allow it to keep you from creating the life of your dreams. I'm living proof of that!

3 MY FIRST TURNAROUND

MY FIRST TURNAROUND

I always give credit to my mother, Nina Mills. I have her last name, not my dad's last name. She had me when she was 16; My mom had my sister when she was 17, two different fathers. I was a mistake. My dad didn't claim me. He said I wasn't his child. Mom hung in there. One of my strong points is my perseverance, and I think I get it from my mom. Through all the crazy stuff in the neighborhood, she just made sure we had.

Many people admire Martin Luther King and Malcolm X and have them as a role model, but for me, it was my mother because she believed it was possible to get out of this place that we were in, she felt that education was the way to do it. Her ambition and her drive to ensure that we had, was amazing to me, whether we were on welfare or Section 8 or what have you, she just always made a way. I appreciated her for that. I respected her and tried to change the paradigm that existed in our family. I wanted to build a better future for us, and bring us to a place where we could say we made it. No one in my family would ever have to experience hurt again, the pain that comes from not being able to provide, or the stress. Many do not know the effects of seeing people die, seeing drug users with needles in their toes when you come out of your house. My mom does not have a ton of degrees; she dropped out of high school to raise me. With or without a diploma, ultimately in that journey, she was always there with me, rooting for me and doing whatever it took to ensure that I wasn't doing anything inappropriate.

I remember coming home from school one day as an eighth grader, and I came back from School. I was tired, and my speech was not necessarily the most fluent. Mom got right to the point and said, "Are you high?" She took me to the doctor and had me drug-tested. And it scared the life out of me, so I never would use drugs because I knew she would take it to that length to ensure that I wasn't.

Once I got to John F. Kennedy High School, I wasn't the most exceptional student. I met coaches and mentors that saw potential in me. I seem to attract the attention of people who wanted more for me than just to teach me a classroom lesson. They were willing to look just a little bit further to see what I needed to be successful.

Looking back on it, I guess they saw promise in me due to the way I respected people or my performance on the football field. I was lucky to meet them. And maybe I was smart enough to be influenced by them instead of other figures around me.

I wasn't all that confident in my abilities because I was getting C's and D's. I thought the school was a joke. Then I got a break. A physics teacher, Mrs. Ranu, who was also the tutor for the football team, made a promise to me. She said that if I committed to studying with her that my SAT score would rise because my verbal score was the issue. And I did it! I committed to it. And she committed to me. She would share things about her family, stuff about her son, stuff that she didn't need to share with me. My score went up significantly from one test to the next because of her. As a junior taking that test, it just amazed me that I was able to do that. And so for the rest of my high school career, I earned straight A's on every report card.

Getting to know Mrs. Ranu and getting smashed in the face with a window frame woke me up. Those events shaped my life. Like Shea Mclean, whom I would not meet for another ten years, I had arrived at a teachable moment. I knew I needed to choose wisely and carefully the things that I was participating in, or I was going to lose my life or go to jail. Period. And I stood by while so many of my friends were getting arrested, just getting taken out of my life. I would go to school, then come back, and they would be gone.

What protected me from that, literally, was football. Football was a savior when I got to high school. Football taught me how to be a leader. The first time I was a leader was as captain of a football team. I realized that kids were listening to me even though we were the same age. Football taught me how to move as a team, as a unit. It taught me how to persevere. It showed me how, in the most terrible situations, like when it's third-and-long, and you're trying to get to the quarterback, now was the time not to be tired. You have to give it your all to get what you need so you can win the game. It taught me to dig-deep no matter how you felt inside because you had a goal to accomplish. It showed me those things.

Football was an excuse, the most significant reason ever because sports were cool, and so was football. So if I wasn't in front of the building where everyone else was hustling and selling drugs and doing a bunch of inappropriate things, I could say I was at football practice. They would say, "Oh, all right. Cool." because they understood that sports were a way to become successful. They would all come to the game to watch me play Friday nights and Saturday mornings.

As much as I admired my mom and as much as she did for me, there was one thing she couldn't provide: a male role model in our home. Sports helped to put that element in my life. I met some good men. It wasn't about race. They were just remarkable men, period. There were black males and multiple white males who wanted nothing more than to see me beat the odds. They wanted me to realize that there were opportunities out there.

Coach Bonadies, Coach Sobota, and Shelton Prescott could get me to run through a brick wall. Each of them had their influence in my life. Coach Bonadies got me set up to understand the importance of football. He also showed me what it took to be an entrepreneur, invested in stocks, and real estate. Also, Coach Bonadies was running the physical education department and was doing things to put his family in a better situation once finished with his career. He had never, ever, hid that, at least from me. Coach Bonadies wanted me to see that there were all sorts of opportunities. He didn't allow me to make excuses for myself. If there were a situation where I couldn't make it, he would come pick me up. He would say, "Don't worry about it; I'll make sure you get a ride every day." What he was doing was allowing me to realize my potential by mitigating any of my excuses from being a member of his football team and I appreciated that. And after he left the coaching position, he placed it in good hands to Coach Sobota, which I can never say enough about, the opportunities he gave me were everything. These opportunities allowed me to stay focused on school and sports, and not the peer pressures that were occurring in my neighborhood on a day-to-day basis. Like being able to buy the clothes that I wanted or to get the sneakers that I wanted when it wasn't coming from my mother rapidly enough. Shelton was like a father figure to me, a role model. He represented everything I wanted to be as an athlete. Shelton played for Syracuse all four years, had some interest from the Dallas Cowboys, and just didn't get drafted after tearing his ACL. He returned to our school after hurting himself. I just wanted to learn everything from him. He was my voice of reason. Anything that I had going on I tried to run past Shelton or Prescott is what we called him. He just seemed to have a good understanding of what we were going through or at least could relate in some way to what we were going through and what was happening at the school. No matter what the conversation was, Prescott always had some great advice on next steps to move a situation forward. It was our talks that made me respect him as a mentor, as a coach, as a teacher, and as this father-like figure helping me navigate life.

At the end of the day, Bonadies was a great mentor. He could teach me things I didn't know. Sabota was the same person, but they were not from my neighborhood nor did they experience poverty at the level I have. Even though I related to them, I didn't feel that they understood what I was genuinely going through growing up in Paterson. Coach Prescott was a product of theirs, meaning he played high school football for them, went to college, graduated from Syracuse, came back, and he began his career as a teacher's aide. They taught him the steps he needed to take to establish himself post-college. I remember them advising him to take a test to get certified as a special needs teacher. Shelton did those things.

He came into my life as my defensive and offensive line

coach. But he grew up in the inner city of Paterson as well. He was a popular person, and people would say that we look alike (that's always a good connection). Shelton just had some inspiring stuff to speak to me at all points of the process, whether in athletics or my role as a substitute teacher. I remember being a substitute teacher and on my first day there wearing a Reggie Miller basketball jersey and a gold chain, which I thought was okay. And I was excited that I had earned enough college credits even to be able to substitute. So to come back to my high school was great. However, those who were working there didn't see it the same way. They saw a young man who hadn't matured enough to know better than to come in dressed like the students. Prescott pulled me to the side in conjunction with Coach Bonadies and said, "Listen, what the hell are you doing? Why would you come into a professional setting with a chain on and a jersey and think that it's okay?" He said, "I spoke to Coach Bonadies, and he explained to me that if you ever show up like that again, you'll never be able to get a job at Kennedy as a substitute teacher. He didn't leave it there, he continued scolding me and taught me what to wear. I was incredibly thankful because at that point I didn't know.

I was a kid from Paterson who dressed like that on a regular basis. I thought that it would be okay to wear a gold chain and jersey because I would be more relatable to the students. Prescott helped me understand that a pair of khakis and a button-up shirt or polo would be more fitting. They need to respect you as someone who is in charge—the authority figure in the classroom and not someone who's their friend and students' view as a get-over. I appreciated that, and I began to change my dress as I walked into the school each day, and it did yield results. Children viewed me more as a leader in the classroom and less as a guy from the neighborhood they know. I was looking for their respect as a professional and less of their connection as a neighborhood celebrity.

I remember Coach Sobota giving me a job doing construction work. He took me out of Checker's, a fast food place near my home in Paterson where I was working. He said, "Come work for me." It was summer work. We did a lot of demolition, a lot of framing, sheetrocking. I was doing all this hard labor for eight dollars an hour — under the table. It was $400 a week; however, after working at checkers, it felt like I was making a million dollars! Coach Sabota would feed me, pick me up for work, and drop me off. Those things were great, but the greatest thing was the things he taught me. We would stop and have lunch. While we were eating, he would give me these jewels, pieces of wisdom. He said, "What I want you to get from this is that you're a smart young man and you don't need to do this for the rest of your life. Your brain should be the driving force. Your brain should work harder than your muscles." And then he began to tell me a story about his dad, and how his dad had worked in construction for, I believe 20-25 years. His dad was able to teach Coach Sobota a ton of things about the job and got him involved in development as well. He said at the end of his career; he had no more feeling in his fingertips from work. Even though he was providing for his family, his dad just didn't have the joy of life anymore because of what he went through to make it that far. That hit home with Sobota and with me as well because I could see the water fill up in his eyes. Though he didn't cry, he just meant that the goal in life is to use your brain and not your brawn. Part of the reason coach chose to become a gym teacher was to begin to make that transition as he had his children. He understood that construction was something he could do on the side, but wanted to be able to enjoy his family, and he had the brains to do so. He became a physical education teacher and did the construction business on the side, and it did not take a daily toll on his life.

It was those experiences that began getting me excited about football. The coaches' dedication to me off the field drove me to work harder to become a better athlete. I remember receiving my first college letters from St. Peter's, an I-AA college. In college sports, are separated into divisions. The highest division is I then there is I-AA, II, and III. For me, this meant that I was one step closer to going to college on a full scholarship and maybe the NFL. I was excited about an I-AA school being interested in me because at the time I was 5-foot-5 and 230 pounds. Just a big ball, yet solid. I began to work harder and grew stronger and before I know it, going into my junior year football season I was weighing 250 bench-pressing 385 pounds, running a 4.95 in the 40-yard dash and I was an animal on the field. I could squat 550 pounds.

This idea of playing in college was real. I was working hard at it and began getting a lot of attention. So going into my senior year, I had a lot of offers. I went on about 20 college visits. I went to schools twice. I went to Howard, Rowan, Marist, and Bryant College. As I was going through the process and not sure where I wanted to go, the deadline for National Letter of Intent had passed. That didn't mean much to me because I did not fully understand the meaning of it. However, I found out it meant all the deals that were on the table were now off the table because they gave the scholarships to other athletes. There were only two schools calling after that date, Rowan and Bryant College, they were still interested. They were walking my paperwork over to specific buildings to get scholarship money so I could attend the university for free. Around April of my senior year, Bryant College called and scheduled a school visit. They said, "Listen, you missed the signing date so the best we can do is $22,000 and you can take $4,000 in loans." My coaches were raving about that, saying, "You better go there. They're the top business schools in the country. I said, "No! What if I drop out? Who will pay the loans back? My coaches said, "That's not you. You're not that kind of person." But I had never been to college. I was the first person in my family to go. I thought maybe I'd get sidetracked, father a child, I just didn't know. I was afraid and did not have many people to talk to about it.
All this opportunity was new, and in a way that was a problem. I was always comfortable with things that

I knew. Even as a kid I never wanted to leave my projects. I didn't want to know what the world had to offer. I just wanted to be in comfortable spaces, no matter how crazy they were. One school I did not visit was Montclair State, a short ride from my home in Paterson. One of the coaches from Montclair State, Coach O'Connor, came to the school to meet me and offered me a financial package that would cover all my expenses. Also, he spoke to me about my remaining scholarship options and explained, "Gemar, I know this seems difficult, but it is not. Think about the things that make you feel the most comfortable and make a decision." After all the exploring and the words of mentors and my mom, three powerful forces came into play. I wanted to stay local because I could still connect with my mom frequently and mentors that helped me to get this far, I wanted familiar surroundings, and I did not want to owe anybody money after college. So I chose Montclair State, not because they gave me the most money, but because all my needs got met by attending the school.

Making that decision to go to Montclair State, or even to go to college in general, was huge. That was the first turnaround. That was the turnaround needed for my family to begin to see the light. Most of the time it was just a celebration for people to have a high school diploma. To be going to college and recognize your family rooting for you, not only my immediate family, like my sisters and my mom but my uncles, my grandparents, my aunts and even my childhood friends, was an accomplishment. Just understanding the things that they had been through, and the things that we had been through together, and the fact that I was going to college, made it even more special. If the story ended there, and life was over, most would say that I was a success, just for being able to navigate the projects through all the trials and tribulations that we went through and being equipped to successfully get out of the Christopher Columbus projects, and go on to a college campus. It was an accomplishment.

4 MAKING IT BIG

MAKING IT BIG

So there I was at Montclair State. Near home or not, I still had a lot to face. I had no car, no job. But what I did have was a refund check. Due to my family's lack of income, I qualified for the maximum amount of financial aid possible from the federal and state government. Moreover, I received scholarships from Montclair State University, which meant that my tuition got overpaid each semester and I would get the remaining balance back in a check. After I bought my books, I'd still have about $3,000 left. That's what happened every four months it is how I survived on a college campus. Each year I earned more and more, even getting a work-study job where I was able to convince Sal, the dean administrative assistant to pay my brother and me $10 an hour. It was a huge deal because everyone one else made $7.25 an hour.

I was a freshman playing football and majoring in computer science. Back then, I was opposed to being an educator. Most of my coaches were educators such as Bonadies, Sabota, and Prescott. One was a physical education teacher, and one was head of the phys ed department, one was a special needs teacher respectively. Their life was pretty good, and they told me, "Consider being an educator because you can navigate that and you'll have people who will support you and make sure you're a success. I still did not agree and continued pursuing computer science as my college major.

I wanted to be a computer science major, yet it seemed like something was preventing me from continuing. I tested into calculus and Computer Science I. It was a good fit except for one thing — I didn't own a computer! It was surprisingly difficult for me to get a grade better than a C. While the semester was going on, I spent my refund check on all insignificant items, and could no longer afford to purchase a laptop. Back then, at the age of 18, I had no understanding of how I should manage my money and priorities. I wasted it all. I would give some to my mom, and then it was just jewelry, clothes, and books for me. I think I spent all the money because I knew there was more coming in four months. I had no concept of saving anything. Lamar, my brother, would say to me, "Why are you doing this? You need to buy a computer." He was saving all of his money, and I was blowing mine. I had every excuse why I should be doing that yet nothing of benefit to show for it. To be honest with you, I was just enjoying having something I never had before. Ultimately, mom struggled to get me the things she thought would keep me motivated to stay in the game of life. So when I received the checks, it was my motivation to never go back to the projects and all the dangers that were there. Nobody ever wanted to be there. It was family oriented, but it was dangerous. People were dying. My friends were getting killed or going to jail. It was a critical situation at every turn.

The result of my poor management of money was to switch my major from Computer Science to math education. I felt like my mentors had a lot to do with why I chose math education versus all the other possible majors and I had to pick math since it has always been my favorite subject to learn in school.

As a math education major, you had to have a specific GPA, and you had to interview to get accepted into the education program. The university required all education majors to complete a full semester of student teaching. They gave us additional educational courses, and it created more opportunities for me to secure more financial aid money. For example, by getting accepted into the school of education and declaring my major as math, I qualified for two scholarships. One was the Urban Teaching Academy where I agreed to teach two years in an urban setting and in exchange the school would pay for all my education courses. Another was a math and science initiative, in which if I agreed to teach math or science in an urban setting they would give me a $1,900 stipend as well as pay for some of my math courses. It is why my senior year refund check, the two times that I received it, was more than $8,000.

Regarding the classroom, Lamar was a huge motivator. When we graduated from high school, he could have gone to Princeton, any school he wanted, to be honest. His GPA was a 3.75. His SAT score was over 1000. He chose Montclair State because I picked Montclair State. We decided to go together and support each other. We're three months apart. He has always been an exemplary student. I was not the best student. We were both afraid because no one in our family had ever been to college. One of the things he would do was keep me on task. We would go to the student center and study in the cafeteria before we went to a party. He had me so disciplined that we'd be in the library until it closed. The cue for us to leave the library was this woman's voice. She would get on the loudspeaker and say, "It is now 11:56. The library closes in four minutes." Lamar was very serious about schoolwork, so serious that he put it as a priority over anything else. As athletes, we had a lot of responsibilities because we received so many perks for being on the football team. I remember a coach asking him, "When are you going to worry about sports as much as you worry about school? Within a week, Lamar quit the team. Lamar said, "For the coach to even say that to him, he didn't care about our future. He only cared about us being able to perform on the football field. There were many situations where there were athletes who were in their fifth year, not nearing graduation, but their eligibility to play football had run out. And there was nothing to be done for them. With Lamar quitting, I continued for about another year, and he would consistently explain to me why he didn't feel like he needed to return. I began to feel the same way through certain experiences. In my junior year, going into my third season, I decided to call it quits. Lamar and I now had more time on our hands. We figured out the lay of the land at the university. We were doing all we had to do, studying and everything. But we had days when we didn't have classes at all, or days when classes started at 4 o'clock. We said, "Hey, we can get jobs." So while we were in school, we began pursuing employment. The best thing I had found that made more money than any other local job that was paying $7.25 an hour and even more than we were making working for Sue over at Morehead Hall was substitute teaching. It was precisely our college major. It gave us a feel for if this was something we wanted to do for the rest of our lives, and they were paying $110 a day! That was much more than anyone else was paying. We began pursuing jobs as substitute teachers in the town where we grew up, which was Paterson.

Both Lamar and I received the job. I found out about the process when I was a sophomore in college. I figured if I worked at, say, Barnes and Noble, I might make $7.25 an hour. But if I could become a substitute, I would be making $110 a day! I did the math on that, and I thought, "I need to be a sub." As soon as I got my 60 credits, I filled out all the paperwork and started subbing in Paterson.

Substitute teaching helped me. It taught me the day-to-day functions of a teacher and helped me understand the things they needed to do. It prepared me for the kind of work I would need to do as an actual certified teacher. It helped me get out in front of a lot of the thought processes that a child would go through, the things that they would do, and how I would be able to stop them and mitigate their disruption to reach them so they could be successful. It also taught me that there were more opportunities outside the classroom to reach children, and ways in which the traditional teacher who kind of went to work and went home was not able to do so. Another thing that I was sure about, and I knew that it had to happen if I wanted to move my family outside the neighborhood we grew up in, was that I had to make more than a base salary. The base salary was only about $37,000. Another thing that substituting let me do was consistently ask questions of people who were holding higher positions and who had risen through the ranks. They had become very successful in the system. I was able to figure out ways to increase my base salary -- what degrees I should pursue. I never knew that if you got a bachelor's degree, you could pursue a Master's in anything you wanted. I learned all that while substituting. I also learned that you would preferably pursue a degree in administration rather than a degree in counseling if you wanted to have an inclusive impact. Both would take two years to earn. But one would open doors for you to run the school building, while the other would only allow you to work with children in a counseling capacity.

Money mattered. I had every intention of being a good teacher, but I also understood that money was essential if I planned to move my family out of our old neighborhood. So when I went into these schools to teach, I wanted to know what opportunities existed that would increase my base salary.

Due to the relationships, I established during substitute teaching; I had identified two employers before I graduated college. The first one was my old high school coaches Shelton Prescott and Frank Bonadies. They knew that I majored in math and thought, "This is an anomaly. You just don't get many black males to teach math in an urban community." I was doing a lot of substitute teaching at Eastside high school in Paterson, and the principal, as well as the chairperson of the department, had offered me a teaching position.

Some people in college dreaded the end of school. They don't like the idea that it's time to go into the real world. Not me. I was so motivated to get on with it. It was way different from when I graduated from high school. I remember not being excited then. College was different. I was so ready to graduate, I told my brother, "I'm never, ever going back to school." In my senior year, I spent time in schools, I was able to speak to administrations and learned ways to add monetary gain to my initial salary. I would even say to people, "I'm going to be a principal." It was pretty contradictory. On the one hand, I told people I wanted to be principal, and on the other, I said I'd never go back to school.

Finally, I got out of college. I graduated, and all those things substituting prepared me for—mentoring, the coaches, the relationships I built within the schools where I had subbed—had all come together. I had finally got employed. I was making $42,000 in base salary as a high school math teacher, and I got an opportunity to be the director of an after-school program at the age of 22. With those two salaries combined, I was making about $75,000 a school year. At that age, I wanted for nothing more. I was living at home with my mom. We were still in Section 8, and I had purchased the car of my dreams. I had the jewelry I always wanted, the success (at least what I had seen in every hip-hop video). I felt that I was doing great, that I had beaten all the odds, and made it to this point where I could celebrate life and be happy that all the hard work from birth to age 22 had paid off. You never know how it's going to play out when you're young with this amount of money, wasting it, enjoying life versus the way people are living their lives on a day-to-day basis. At age 22, I was a success. I had it made. Now a true professional in the field of education, I thought I had escaped the projects for good. Soon I learned that it's not quite that easy.

5 A NARROW ESCAPE

A NARROW ESCAPE

Along with my career success came financial reward as well. It's fair to say I was making more than most people in Paterson, almost definitely than anyone in my part of town. My background did not prepare me for earning large amounts of money at such a young age. There were lots of things I wanted, things I'd never had. Like flashy jewelry and a nice car.

There's a book written by Malcolm Gladwell called "Blink," and in one of the chapters, he speaks about stereotypes, and how stereotypes rule the world. Despite what your attributes are, despite the best-case scenario, once people have judged you in the blink of an eye, ultimately, they stick you in that box forever. And

I felt like coming from the community that I grew up in, had troubles in, coming from the projects, going to school, people knew me to be this one type of person. My nickname was "Biggie." That's what everyone called me. They didn't call me by my real name. And growing up, you go through phases of life, the wants, the haves, the have-nots, you do things people don't agree with like, buy jewelry. Jewelry was my thing. I regularly had huge chains. I was always into the flash and hip-hop culture. But I was also 15, right? And by the time I became an adult at 22, I was making the most money in my household, and I still thought I needed those things to feel like I was successful. I purchased a particular car. And despite me having a career, making more than $75,000 a year, people still believed I was doing inappropriate things to get the money to purchase the stuff that I had.

Even though I woke up every day at 6 o'clock in the morning to go to work an administrator, who was a former high school teacher, happened to be my principal. From my high school days, she and the gym teacher knew me to be a very flashy, smart young man, but still influenced by the friends I kept. They nevertheless judged me based on those friends.

The friends with whom the district tended to associate me with had a reputation that preceded them in the streets. It was different from the notoriety I was trying to build, which was creating something in which children would see the value of education and the cool in it. Like, how cool would it be to go to college and graduate and get a great job and be successful? Versus how cool is it to hang in the streets, hustle, whether it be drugs or illegal items that were stolen from somewhere, to make you feel that you have it all? I always felt this incident carried me into adulthood. I was working at an elementary school for Paterson Public schools, doing great work. My evaluations were amazing. I was doing my best. It was my first year ever teaching, I was out of college, making excellent money and I wanted to see my students achieve. I was preparing fifth-graders. Some of them were considered to be among the most challenging children. I was excellent with them, and my observations said that. Then a video came out, and it nearly wrecked everything I had been trying to build. This video had some inappropriate activities on it. And I would agree. In hindsight, it wasn't the best for me to be in, but I wasn't the person perpetuating the negativity.

This documentary was chronicling more of the negative qualities of the city, sensationalizing what a community would not want to be known for, such as criminal activity and gang culture. The things that any mayor or school superintendent would not associate. The video was a local thing where people began to pick up cameras and document all the foolishness that was going on in the neighborhood. The people who created the video saw it as entertainment. The police didn't see it that way.

The people featured in the video were saying unsettling things. Like, "If somebody has a problem with me I can have 50 people at your doorstep." All things that would instill fear in the average person in the community and at some point near the end I plug into this documentary.

"Yeah, you know, this is our guy, he's doing good things," they said. "He does what he's gotta do." Back then, jewelry was my thing. So I had this huge chain. It was bigger than anybody's chain in the community. It was a big G chain, and I was telling them, "Look at what we're doing. We're opening up a store. We're building up the community." I was saying that stuff on camera. But I guess the person watching was thinking, "Well, we don't see that. And this is not a community space for kids. These are a bunch of grown men, and just 30 minutes ago we saw someone with a shotgun."

At the time I was oblivious to all of this stuff. I had no clue what was in the video before the point where I appeared in it. I was thinking that my friends were doing something to promote the store that they opened, to shine a light on the positive things that were happening in the community. Documentaries in the neighborhood were not unfamiliar. It is what was going on in popular hip-hop culture. For me, it was, "Let's come in and talk about successful things that are happening." But when I saw the video, I thought, "Oh, man. I hope I don't get into any trouble."

I wasn't aware that someone had an illegal firearm or that people had their faces tied up with bandana's to conceal who they were. I went and got a copy of it. I didn't have to look far. To everyone in the neighborhood, it was entertainment. It started with rap battles, and then it turned to documenting lifestyles. For everyone who was in the know, it was a joke, just people being funny. But to the outside world, it was, "Oh, no! Gang recruitment. It is an initiation; this is instilling fear into the community and gaining power on the streets." That's what the police were saying. They had no other interpretation of what this was.

I'm not 100 percent sure how it went, but I do know there was a person at the beginning of the movie with the people, with the guns, and he worked in schools. He had lost his job, and some of the people he connected with were very connected to my principal's best friend. His name was Coach Harvey. I'm sure they shared with him that this person had gotten into trouble from the video, and they were trying to get him his job back, and then the conversation probably went something like, "Oh, Gemar's in the video, and nothing happened to him." And he shared that information with the principal, who now has this vendetta to make sure I receive a reprimand for being in the documentary. Even though I wasn't near a gun nor near any negative stuff the principal relentlessly pushed until something happened.

I got to school, worked like a typical situation. It was a few weeks since the person got in trouble for what he did when I got called down to the office, where they gave me a letter. They told me to report to the central office instead of the school on Monday at 9 a.m. I said okay, and they wanted me to sign that I received the letter. When I went upstairs and opened the note, it said my job was in jeopardy for conduct unbecoming, and that I would need to report to the school district for a conference and that my union rep would be present to hear everything that was to occur.

At that moment, I replayed my entire life in my head. Watching all my hard work and all the temptations and dangers I had avoided to even get into a college, to get a degree in math, to get a certification, only to have someone to say, "We're about to take all this away." And that's what they were saying because "conduct unbecoming" is one of those accusations for which they can take away your certification forever. I knew I hadn't done anything wrong; I knew I wasn't the person that they were painting me to be. But again, when we talk about what Malcolm Gladwell said about stereotypes, it just seemed like my association with my friends in high school carried over to their beliefs about who I was as a person. They had judged and classified me, and they didn't give me a real chance to show them who I was.

A few hearings ensued. We went back and forth. The superintendent wouldn't budge. He said he believed it was true, that what the principal was claiming, that the video they saw was nothing short of some form of intimidation tactic toward the neighborhood, and since I am in it at some point, I shouldn't work with children.

I read the Bible every day, looking for guidance. I'd spent four years of my life in college to earn this rigorous degree, and now someone was telling me that it was all for nothing. I no longer had football to pursue a career in education. I was distraught. But one of the things I did not do was quit. As I said, perseverance is a quality of mine. I refused to give up.

Even though we were going through this horrible situation with the school district, I put my resume into Passaic, a nearby school district. I put it into Newark, too. I put it into any neighboring school districts so at least I could substitute while this went on, but I refused to just tuck my tail between my legs. I don't know where I learned that, but I completely understood failure was not an option. In the midst of the hearings, I ended up getting a substitute job in Passaic and a couple of interviews for full-time positions.

I'll never forget what happened next. I had been meeting with a trustworthy lawyer for three months, and we had gone over the entire case. Now the hearing day was coming close. Then, the day before the hearing, my lawyer called and said he had to do a trial, so another lawyer named would substitute for him. He explained, "We would meet in the coffee shop before going into the hearing." A brief meeting in the coffee shop for a case that would determine my future? I was thinking, "I'm done. I don't know what's going to happen."

I had a conversation with my mother. She said, "you pray on it, and then you go, and you deal with it because you know you did no wrong." I went there and met the new lawyer. We had a 15-minute conversation inside a coffee shop right outside the board of education. Then we headed toward the hearing, just a few steps away. As we walked in, my lawyer and the district's lawyer met. I went in and waited.

Then my lawyer called me outside. He said, "They were ready for a battle." That guy is the lead partner for the firm that the district hired. He's not the normal person who would fight these cases. They talked, my lawyer, came back out and said, "Listen, they want to settle." The other attorney said to my lawyer, "We're gonna try to rectify this because it's not that serious and only gonna cost us more money." Both lawyers left the room for about 15 minutes.

My lawyer came back in and said, "Look. The district said they'll give you your year of service experience. They will pay you back pay from February up until June, and redact all allegations from my record if you agree not to sue them for defamation of character." I said, "Okay," because I just wanted to be done. Plus, I had just received information from Newark public schools that I was going to get the job at East Side High School in Newark, NJ. They drew up the contract right then and there. I signed the agreement not to sue them, received all of my back pay and my year of experience, and got an opportunity to get my old job back. I told them no! If I needed to go through all this to prove my character, then this is not a place I want to be. It left a bad taste in my mouth that in the place where I was born and raised, and in the area where I desired to provide all my services it had come to this. But it was my destiny because I never looked back, and I dedicated my heart and my soul to the children of Newark.

What I learned from this is that perception is extremely powerful; who you associate with, and what you do when you're with them, is very important. So I would tell anyone never denounce your friends. However, when you get in front of a camera or you get an opportunity to speak, speak truth to power. Let people know that you do not agree with what it is that's occurring and make sure your beliefs shine through.

It is the stuff that may be affecting us for centuries that needs to change. Ultimately if we can realize people, minorities in general in inner cities, that these behaviors only add to the destruction of who we are and don't necessarily add value to our real power and our ability to build great things in the world.

6 CAREER TAKEOFF

CAREER TAKEOFF

After that whole ordeal in Paterson went down, I began working in the Newark public school system. I started at East Side as a math teacher. It was a very diverse school, all I would say it was a melting pot, as many races as there possibly could be. There were blacks, Portuguese, Ecuadorians, Brazilians, Peruvians, Puerto Ricans, Dominicans, etc. I just thought it was amazing the way the school functioned and the various ways races pulled from each other's cultures. I saw the young black men wearing tight clothes, while some of the young Hispanic men wore fitted caps and dressing hip-hop like and speaking the language of most hip-hop artist. That was something I hadn't experienced in my earlier years or college, probably because the interaction was limited. As a teacher, I had to interact with everybody, because I got looked at as a role model and I wanted to know where my students were from, what type of life they lived, what culture they experienced in their families. Those things were important to me as I interacted with and related to them. It was a very proud school. Many staff members had graduated from the school and had come back to work at East Side. I thought that was a fantastic thing for the community.

It was a huge school, the most comprehensive high school in Newark, housing 1,700 students. It wasn't performing at its best when I got there yet began doing better. Not only because of me but because of the hard work of the principal there, the administration, the students dedicating themselves to it, the teachers showing up to get it done, in 2009 the school was ranked the highest, regarding performance, of all comprehensive high schools in Newark. That was amazing, to come from a place of failure to compete with many of the magnet schools that have a selection process for children.

I taught first-year students to begin, and the following year the administration gave me the junior class students who had failed geometry. Now I was working with the lowest performing students in the school in regards to standardized test performance and GPA. My chairperson must have seen something in me. He would comment on the way I craft my lesson plans. He felt that my level of planning wasn't something he was seeing from the other teachers. One day he even asked me where I'd learned to put lesson plans together. I told him that my planning stemmed from my students' needs. I would look through the textbook and try to anticipate things they were going to have trouble with; I wanted to ask them questions that would challenge their thinking without overpowering them and cause anxiety.

We had a challenge. The school test scores were sitting at around 43 percent in mathematics, and we needed to be somewhere around the 60s because East Side was a school that was being reborn. The school had experienced some troubles and hired a new principal just a year or so before, and they saw progress. With me having the partially proficient students I knew a good percentage of them needed to pass. It would increase our changes because the other teachers worked with some of the stronger skilled students. Well, of my 80 students, about 60 percent of them passed the test, and with those numbers and what the other teachers contributed, we were around 69 percent proficiency for mathematics in one year. I got a lot of praise for the success of the students and felt that I could do more. In the midst of my stay at East Side, I began pursuing my Masters. My goal was to become a principal. I didn't know then that I wasn't ready for that, but I wanted to do it fast. So I searched online for programs that offered accelerated programs and found American Intercontinental University, which had an intense 18-month program.

For me taking classes online was difficult. There's

not much support in place. You read it, you know it, and you put it back on paper, in proper English form, and you pretty much get a grade. There's no one to coach you through it. There are no do-overs. There's not much in the way of extra resources, whereas in a traditional school there is tons of support. There are tutoring programs. There are people to work with you face to face. The distant learning forced me to do all the work and not cut corners. I retained more of my Master's coursework than I grasped in my bachelor's degree. My master's program forced me to be an independent learner. I had to learn the coursework, and there was no one to help me. There was no class group to take on some of the questions. The assignments were unambiguous, you had to respond to them on a weekly basis, and if you didn't do it, then you got the grade you earned, which was an F.

What I learned above all was I began to believe in my abilities to figure things out. I started to think that whatever I thought was possible could be done if I wanted it to; I remember my brother saying something like, "You can't be an architect," and me telling him, "If that's what I wanted to do, I could be that. It's just not something I'm passionate about." I remember telling him that if I wanted to be a doctor, I could be that. However, I chose to do education and sticking with it because it is my greatest passion.

On June 10th, 2007 I earned my Masters. I went to my graduation in Chicago and was ecstatic. I let my chairperson, know that I'd obtained my Masters in

Education Leadership and wanted to be a principal. He advised me to take some intermediate steps on the way to the position. I began teaching Algebra I in summer school at Barringer High School that July. The assistant superintendent of all the high schools would come into my classroom regularly. He always had these crazy challenges. One of them was for me, as a summer school math teacher. I was required to go to all of the other summer school math teachers and pull their assessment data for the week. To determine, which students were the highest performers and what their likelihood of passing the class was based on what they had done thus far. I was not in charge of these teachers, but he had challenged me to figure out who was on target to pass. Everybody knew the assistant superintendent was this wild, crazy person who got things done for children. Thus everyone still loved him despite his behavior sometimes. I had high respect for him, and of course, I did the challenge. Thankfully, the teachers bought into what I was trying to do, and they turned over their results. I was able to get them to do the scoring of their data, and then turn it over to me including the names and the averages of their students. Then one day the assistant superintendent came to my classroom while I was teaching. He walked in and said, "Where are your kids' tests?" He began going through their portfolios and wanted to know how they had performed. He told me to submit the data to him. I aggregated it and sent it. He was impressed by what my kids were able to do. He ended up coming back and asked me what I was doing to get this particular group of students to perform this way. I told him I was building rapport with them and planning lessons to try and anticipate their learning gaps. I had questions and assignments prepared for that. We did mini-lessons on skills they were lacking.

That conversation led to a talk with my chairperson. I told him I wanted to pursue a chairperson job. He said, "I don't want to see you go, but I have an opportunity for you. He called Arts High School to speak to their vice principal, who was a former math teacher at East Side High School. I didn't know the vice principal, and I had never met him. He connected me with Mrs. White, who was the principal of Arts at the time. My chairperson made the call and said, "We got a young guy (I had just turned 25), and he's interested in being an administrator. And I think he can do it. Here's what he did for us at East Side." At the interview, Mrs. White, the principal, told me I was going to be in charge of science and math, not just math. She told me there would be challenging events and challenging teachers. All I kept saying was, "Whatever I don't know I'll learn." The thing that got me to this place so quickly was my willingness to work for 24 hours to get information, whereas most people would just wait 24 years to gain this experience. So I would work relentlessly to try to catch up to counterparts who were 15 or 20 years in the game. That was the only way I could do it. I think she bought into that. She offered me the job at Arts High School to be the chairperson of mathematics and science.

She submitted my paperwork to the assistant

superintendent in charge of high schools. A few days later, I received an email from the assistant superintendent saying he would like to meet, because he had a plan, and it wasn't Arts High School. I went there, and there was a man named Henry McNair, who was going to be the vice principal at Shabazz, and Allison Devaughn, who was scheduled to be the chairperson of language arts at Shabazz. The assistant superintendent said, "Do you know why you're here?" I was assuming we were going to have a follow-up meeting for the chairperson position. I said, "I'm thankful for the opportunity to be an administrator. Where I go doesn't matter to me because I plan to effect change wherever I am." That was me being the nice guy. The assistant superintendent responded by saying, "Good because you're going to Shabazz!"

7 SHABAZZ

SHABAZZ

A few years ago, if you were to walk into Shabazz High school, your reaction would have been, "What the heck is going on? Is this a school? Why are kids fighting so much? Why is it such a hostile and volatile environment? Why are 20 kids just sitting in the hallway?"

Well, to tell you the truth, it wasn't that bad it was worse. In fact, when you look back a few years at the statistics, you might wonder why anyone would want to be in charge of Malcolm X Shabazz High School.

In 2009-10, there was 119 fire alarm pulls and 25 in-school arrests. In 2010-11, teachers issued 1,492 F's on first quarter report cards, and only 20 of 810 students made the honor roll. At one point the school ranked 314 out of 328 in New Jersey, with a math proficiency of 19% and a graduation rate of 63%.

But this story isn't really about statistics. It's about people. There was a great young man at Shabazz. His nickname was Bullet. He would tell people that I was his dad because his build was like mine and his facial features were like mine. He was a thrilled, energetic young man and incredibly charismatic. So much so that at the age of 17 he had a 22-year-old girlfriend whom he had children with, and he just loved to be at school. He would come regularly. He liked to joke, but a good kid. And he graduated.

He would stop by periodically after graduation and say, "I need a job." And I told him he had to quit smoking weed. "Bullet," I told him, "you can't come to ask me for a job, and you smell like a pound of weed. Can't do that." So he would laugh it off. I would say, "You graduated, we were able to accomplish that let's keep the momentum going. Then Christmas came. I was watching the news, and they said a shooting occurred at Slick's nightclub in nearby Irvington, N.J. The owner's cousin or brother or someone like that got murdered. So was another man. For about a day they didn't know who the shooter was. It turns out; the killer was Bullet. Not only did he kill the owner's relative, but he also shot his friend. They said he was so high on drugs that he didn't know what was going on. To this day, he's in jail for murder.

Though this was a tragic story not everyone's was like Bullet's, there were other stories, many of them harrowing. Something at Shabazz had to change. You could even say that most things had to change. Seymour Sarason, a pioneer in the field of community psychology, said, "If you want to change and improve the climate and outcomes of schooling—both for students and teachers, there are features of the school culture that must change, and if they do not, your well-intentioned efforts will be defeated."

Those words made an impression on me. Even if you made a point of doing things right, you would fail unless you did the right things. But what were the right things?

Let's go back to the beginning. Shabazz is one of the oldest schools in Newark, built in 1913. Over the decades, Newark's demographics changed, so much so that in 1972, South Side became Malcolm X Shabazz High School, named after the Muslim minister and human rights activist who had gotten assassinated seven years earlier. In the years between the death of Malcolm X and the naming of the school after him, racial rioting tore apart large areas of Newark. Today, there is only one Malcolm X Shabazz High School in the country — and it's in Newark.

Some great people have graduated from Shabazz. They include the former mayor of Newark, Sharpe James; and the former superintendent, Marion Bolden; Lonnie Wright, who once played pro football and pro basketball in the same season; Ed Koch, former mayor of New York City; and N.J. State Senator Ron Rice.

When I arrived at Shabazz, it was in the worst of stages. I'm talking about 1,500 students. There were fights regularly, and it wasn't safe. The fire alarm would get pulled two or three times a day, and children would run outside to get weapons that they had stashed. We were dealing with some severe situations. I can recall one year going out for a fire alarm and then having someone shoot off rounds on the football field as we left the building.

As time went on, things at Shabazz got worse and worse. I remember one of the guidance counselors looking at me and saying, "You think you can fix this?" At the time I was just the chairperson of math. I was working extremely hard just to try to salvage something because I knew kids' lives were at stake.

In 2008 -2009 the principal, was a very immeasurable leader who didn't have much support. The assistant superintendent's idea was to provide the support with some new energy in relevant areas. That would take some of the workloads of the principal. The kids loved and respected her, but she wasn't getting the results the district was looking for fast enough. The 1,500 students respecting only one person led to constant turmoil at the school. At the time I was 25 years old; I think they ultimately took a risk, saying, "Let's stick Gemar over there. What's the worst that could happen? We'll put him with a group of people who are seasoned administrators." On September 5, 2008, the students arrived, and the new administrative team of Malcolm X Shabazz high school went to work.

By the end of 2008 - 2009, I had done some excellent work with teachers. However, the school was still in turmoil. At the end of that school year, the principal received a transfer to West Side High School, and the school district hired a new principal at Shabazz. I was able to rid the system of five teachers who were not suitable for children. It was a lot of long nights to accomplish that task. Getting rid of a teacher is not something you brag about, but at the end of the day, there are people in the system that are indeed, destroying children. You must understand that we spend eight hours of the day with the students. There are only 16 hours that you're awake. Most people get eight hours of sleep. Schools receive half of a child's waking hours. We cannot allow a staff member to fill that time with nonsense, or let a classroom to be so crazy that the students never learn anything for four years; you're destroying those children.

There were a lot of feedback conferences, a lot of coaching—because I think that support is of the utmost importance—and observations in those classrooms. That's why I can say I've never, ever had a teacher leave my office infuriated with my leadership, saying, "I hate him, he did me wrong." I would give them so much attention that if it didn't work, they understood that it wasn't because I gave up on them. Nevertheless, the impact of lesser performing staff that includes, teachers, administrators, and support staff, lead to mass amounts of inconsistency with students. The lack of consistency resulted in fights, fire alarm pulls, student lack of respect for the workers, and poor academic performance.

Here's a story, maybe the craziest Shabazz story ever. It began with surgery, followed by a robbery, and wound up with a kid almost dying in school. Our principal had to go in for surgery. We didn't know what the operation was, but she explained to us, the administration, that we must ensure that students are safe in her absence. We felt her surgery profoundly. She was so powerful, like cartoon powerful, if there was a melee in the hallway and she was walking out of her door backward, by the time she turned around, the corridors would be apparent. She was that powerful. You could hear the kids saying, "she's coming!"

In her absence, the vice principal was in charge. He was the senior administrator. The next day we came to school, and I have never seen anything like it in my life. We had a half-day, and the Twilight Program had a half day as well. The Twilight Program was a night school program for students who were over age and under-credited. Many of the district's most problematic students were in the program. I was walking the halls around 10 am clearing them when I saw two guys I didn't recognize. "Hey," I said, "Where's your class?" They laughed and ran off. I was on a walkie-talkie while chasing them down the stairs. They got into the cafeteria, hopped behind the lunchroom counter and stole money from the cash register.

Then around 11 am, I heard chatter in the hallway, a lot of chatter. About 100 students were congregating in the hallway. I told them they had to go to class, and they went running like a stampede. It sounded like horses running through the hall. They played a game called chase. They would run up, and they would run down. If the administration were at this end, they would run the other way. If security were at this end, they would run the other way. Up and down. At some point, I got the call: Code One, Code One. That meant there was a fight. By the time I got downstairs, one of the other administrators was there. They had beaten this student senseless. We weren't sure if he was going to make it. An incident like that shouldn't have gone unsupervised for that long. So we went to the surveillance video to see what happened. It was the craziest thing. A teacher had come out of her room, saw them fighting, went back into her room and closed the door. She didn't call an administrator, and she didn't call the office, she didn't do anything. She just let it be. Just adding to the mindset of, "it is what it is."

The principal left after that year. I was still the chairperson of math. A new principal got hired, and the vice principal wasn't fond of our new leader. She had many demands and caused the vice principal anxiety. At the time, the vice principal was having some heart trouble, and he had to get a pacemaker put in. He went out without finishing the master schedule. So we had one-on-ones with the principal. And during my one-on-one, the principal said, "Gemar, you're a math person. You should be able to do the schedule. They tell me you enjoy it." Well, I wasn't sure who told her that, but okay. I had been working with the vice principal to try and learn the schedule. At the time I didn't have any tenure, so I just said, "Of course. Whatever you need from me." I knew nothing about scheduling except what I had done with the vice principal. There were three weeks left before school opened and no master schedule.

I worked from eight in the morning until about two in the morning for three weeks straight to build the master schedule from scratch. Everyone said it wouldn't get done. Everybody! What the principal wanted did not go with what the vice principal had built. So I had to delete it and start over. George, a person from the district who managed the schedule, told me that if I destroyed the master schedule, there would be no time to get it done.

I learned, and I listened to the principal, ensuring that the master schedule reflected her request. She brought some assistants to help me with the master schedule. We got it all on paper, and I plugged it into the system, and I ran it. It was at 50 percent, which meant I still had 800 kids to create schedules by hand because the program didn't do it by itself. And I went to work. I went three weeks non-stop. On Day 1 of school opening, guess what? All the students had a schedule, and the principal was excited, and the teachers and the administrative team had a nickname for me. They said, "Here's the Golden Boy. He did that for the principal. He can do no wrong." Someone once told me that I have a knack for doing things that no one else thinks can be done. I guess that's true. I am not sure where that comes from, yet I think it stems from my childhood; this recurring theme of getting stuff done when people tell you it's not possible.

Being the Golden Boy was dying fast because the principal was the devil in of the teaching staffs eyes. They hated this woman! It was a shame because she taught me how to be an administrator. She taught me how to document, how to manage a person. She taught me how to rid the system of a person who is not suitable for children. I embraced the knowledge she had, and I could see, based on the support documents that she would provide for us, that she had a working understanding of what it took to run a good school.

The principal's teachings coupled with my innate ability to engage in rigorous conversation without creating animosity lead to better outcomes for students. I will never forget working with a math teacher, in my department, who was having some trouble with the students. I would work with him regularly. We had a feedback conference. I told him, "I've been in your class twice, maybe four times, some walkthroughs and observations, what is it that you need from me? Because I've been putting all this stuff in writing, giving you action plans, supporting you with discipline and anything you've asked." He said, "I just want you to leave me alone and let me do it." And I said, Okay, would you please write what you're saying in this document? He said it was no problem, and he wrote down, "I don't need any more support from Mr. Mills. I just need to focus on what I gotta do, and I'll get it done." At the end of the year, he got rated unsatisfactory because he didn't improve. Sometime later, the district's lawyers called me and said I needed to go to court because he was on trial for tenure charges. It was my first tenure hearing as an administrator. So the morning came, and I was preparing to head to the court, and the district lawyer called. He said I didn't have to show up because the document that the teacher signed, the one saying he didn't need any support, was something the teacher's union couldn't fight, and that the teacher was going to lose his tenure.

Also, I recall a challenging conversation I had with a non-tenured teacher whom I got informed he would not be able to return to Newark as a teacher because he did not have what it took to move student achievement in Newark Public Schools. I explained that he should consider working in another school district. After the conversation with the teacher and I expressed my concerns. We went through the artifacts I'd collected, line by line. Once the conference was over, he looked me in the eye and said thank you. "Thank you for all of the things that you've done for me. I understand why I got the rating that I received, and you are a great leader. I appreciate you, and I'm sure I'll see you again."

I haven't seen him, but he has reached out to me to tell me how he was doing in the other district. He was doing pretty well. I thought he was a capable teacher but the children of Newark were just too aggressive for him.

The aggression would create fear in teachers, which they would sense, and become remarkably disrespectful to him and he would lose control. It always amazes me when my colleagues on the administration would say, "You have a gift to tell somebody to go eat s@&! and they would smile and eat it. It makes me laugh." They were saying that I could have difficult conversations that most people would have and it would become a very toxic situation where nothing gets accomplished. But I could persevere through that, telling people some very troubling stuff. We're talking about teachers making $100,000 a year, and I'm telling, "I don't know what they've been doing with you for the last 25 years, but this is not good for our students." "You're not moving the needle, and here's why. The teachers would listen, take it, and say, "Okay, I'm gonna get better." And as long as I kept my end of the bargain I never ran into a situation where someone attacked me or felt like they needed to get revenge because I did somebody wrong. I was always transparent.

However, the principal struggled to build rapport with her staff or maybe it was not significant to her. She had a great harmony with most of the children and a very poor rapport with most of the teachers. It is not an ideal way to run a school. I have learned that if adults don't like you, then they speak those evils to the children, and the students just carry out their actions. And here's an example of that.

The state of New Jersey sent a team to audit Shabazz high school. By then we were down to about 1,100 kids because parents were transferring their children out left and right. We were into our second principal in two years, and the state team was interviewing the students, asking them what they thought of Shabazz. One of them replied, "This is my school. We run this shit." A student told a state monitor that the students were running the school.

During the state team's visit, the kids were setting fires in the bathroom, pulling the fire alarm on a regular basis, and cursing at the people from the state as they walked the hallways, asking them why they were here. The visit occurred during the winter months; it was snowing outside. A student pulled the fire alarm. As we all exited the building, the state monitors were pelted with snowballs and ran back inside for shelter. They were supposed to spend five days with us. On the fourth day, they gave us a draft report and did not return on the fifth. They recommended that Shabazz close as soon as possible and the school district should start over.

Instead, the district decided to replace the principal and apply for a *"School Improvement Grant,"* which would give an additional $6 million over three years to help turn around the school. This principal would have more autonomy than the previous ones, as well as more resources to get the job done with students. It was sad to say that despite being awarded the grant money the same conditions persisted, the same types of stories over and over about students wreaking havoc on the building, and adults not able to control them.

More stories about fire alarms getting pulled, students assaulting other students, and students getting arrested and staff simply saying, "It is what it is."

One day I was in the central office. The principal was in her office, and I heard a commotion outside. I walked out of my room, and about ten students were sitting on the chairs located in the school's central office. There were two teachers at the counter, and they were telling the students, "You have to go because there are parents in the office." I came out and told the students, "We not having this. You gotta go." They left. Then a parent said, "This is ridiculous. Where is the principal?" The teacher pointed at me and said, "Do you want the real principal? Or do you want the lady in that office?" And I would consistently say, "Don't do that, because I'm in full support of the principal in that chair. And I don't want to make it seem like I'm advocating or soliciting anybody to promote me into her position because I don't want it."

Everyone would say, "You should be the principal." I still wasn't sold. But I would get thoughts about what I would do IF I ever were to become principal. I couldn't help thinking, "If they just did this, maybe that would work."

When that year ended, that principal too was removed. A new superintendent came in, and we didn't know what was going to happen with Shabazz. All I knew was we were without a principal. I was now the vice principal, doing whatever work was asked of me by the executive administration to ensure that when students returned in September of 2011, there was some sense of normalcy. What they had experienced for the last three years was not something that any parent would wish on their child.

8 PRINCIPAL

PRINCIPAL

I wanted no part of being the principal. I had watched Shabazz disintegrate. However, my work with the school's master schedule got the attention of the assistant superintendent. While the school district was searching for a new principal, I was contacted to open the school building and to build the master schedule.

During the summer months, the horror stories from the school year lingered. Students were said to be out of control, and teacher attendance rates were at an all-time low. Staff members shared their memories of a former Superintendent and Shabazz alumni's visit to Shabazz in late June. They explained, "the former Superintendent toured the entire school speaking to them." She asked two specific questions, "how can we fix this?" and "who can we get to fix it?" Many staff members responded to her questions with one answer, "Make Mr. Mills the principal!" I remember seeing the former Superintendent exiting the school on that day in June and wiping tears from her eyes due to the conditions of the school she once attended.

As the summer days continued so did the rumors. I heard stories from some state officials who had visited Shabazz and even custodial workers within the district that I was going to get the principal job. The rumors went from "Mr. Mills is going to be the principal" to "Mr. Mills is the new principal at Shabazz", which was incredibly frustrating. Here I was, not even confident I would be willing to pursue the job, and everyone was congratulating me. Alumni were reaching out to me, asking if I'd received a call. I told them no. The first day of school was getting closer and closer, yet no principal had got selected.

Around the second week of August, I decided to apply and interview for the job. My decision had nothing to do with adults and all to do with students. I was facilitating senior orientation, and a student raised her hand and asked, "Who is our principal?" I explained that one had not got selected. The student responded, "Why can't you be our principal?" I said, "I do not make that decision however if I were your principal I would not tolerate the negative behaviors that you all have displayed during my tenure at Shabazz." A young man yelled out from across the room and said, "That's what we need!" and because of those words, I decided to pursue the principal vacancy at Shabazz high school.

I begin planning in my mind what my playbook would look like and simultaneously I was talking myself into not taking the job. I started to feel like I was being set up. I couldn't make real decisions from the place I was in, and I needed to stop thinking as if I were the principal. I didn't want to have a conflict of interest when the new principal arrived. I was stuck in a catch-22, opening the school building and handle the day-to-day task of the principal yet not the actual principal.

The Superintendent had not offered me the principal job after taking part in her eight-hour interview, which consisted of many components. I went through the process in mid-July of 2011 and had only received a phone call from one of Shabazz's Alumni Association members. The alumnus explained, "that of the 50 candidates, only four made it through." I was one of the four because I earned a B-rating on the Superintendent interview rubric. Nevertheless, the Superintendent was looking for an A-rated principal. She felt that Shabazz was the worst school in the district and the worst in the state, so why would she put a B-rated person in the worst of situations? Her logic was simple: "If you're not an A-rated principal, I'm not going to put you in the worst school, because you're not prepared. I need an A." I received this news, and I thought, "It is what it is. I guess I'm not going to get the job. I'm happy being a vice-principal because there are less responsibility and more opportunity. I'm fine with that." I was happy with being a scheduler.

The week before school opened, I got a call to come downtown to meet the Superintendent. She asked me what I thought about the interview process. I told her I thought I did well in most of the components but not all. She wanted to know what I thought my weaknesses were. I mentioned my ability to communicate in such a way that people could understand what I was trying to convey to them. She pressed me on it. I said, "I'll read more. I'll learn the jargon that the staff is familiar with so I can be sure they can understand what I'm saying. I could use some help in identifying what professional development teachers need."

"I can support you with that," she said.

At the end of the conversation, she told me, "If you had said anything else, I wouldn't have chosen you."

So I guess I hit it right on the nose.

It ended with this sentence: "I want to offer you the position of principal at Malcolm X Shabazz High School."

Then she shook my hand and sent me into a room with her assistant superintendent. What he had to say was not a pretty picture. He talked about the 30 teacher vacancies, the administrative vacancies and critical areas like language arts and mathematics. He gave me advice on how to proceed. I listened, like I do with everything, and took the pieces that were important to me and then put it into something I'd been putting together: a 90-day plan.

I was elated. It was late August, a week before school was going to open, and I had already thought this stuff through. I'm thinking; I've got to get in touch with these people and put them in place because I'm going to be principal! I remember getting to Shabazz, and the principal from Boys Latin Prep Charter, with whom I was working to build his master schedule, was in the office. So was my sister, Natica, because I was helping her make the master schedule for Barringer. I walked toward the central office where they were sitting. They got up to walk me to my old room, which was behind the main office counter and to the right. Instead, I turned left and opened the principal's door, and took a seat in the principal's chair. I just said to my sister and the principal from Boys Latin Prep come into the office. Their eyes lit up. That was how I let them know.

PART TWO
GOLD

9 GETTING STARTED

GETTING STARTED

Suddenly I knew how a new president must feel. It's one thing to campaign, to make promises and to offer policy proposals. It's another thing entirely to sit down in that chair for the first time, knowing that your every word and action meant something, knowing that when the phone rings at three in the morning, it's for you.

In much the same way, thinking about what you might do as principal and then getting the chance to do it are two different things. There's a big difference between having some colleagues think you might make a good principal and then sitting down and having to become one.

History was against me, and not just recent Shabazz history. There was also a deep and intimidating history in the larger picture. For decades educators have searched for the cure for student failure within urban school districts. Despite the many antidotes prescribed by some of education's best and brightest scholars, the problems still exist and in most cases have become worse.

To think that I could solve these longstanding problems within 180 days might seem to an outsider to be the height of arrogance. I had three things going for me:

1. I knew the intricacy because I had lived it.
2. There was nothing to lose. The state already wanted to close the school. There was nowhere to go except up.
3. I had discovered some valuable resources in books. One of them would become vital in those six precious days between the time I got hired and the time we could open our doors in September.

This much I knew: Two major issues affecting Shabazz were the culture within it and the quality of the instruction delivered to students. How should any principal attack these problems? Choosing one can be a mistake, yet attempting both could prove overwhelming. It was a tough decision that I was forced to make in a short period. The fate of the school, and the future of hundreds of students hung in the balance. I was lucky. My gut told where to begin, and I had an ally in Michael Fullan, a best-selling author and an expert on educational reform. We were both focusing on the same word "culture!"

You can see Fullan's beautifully expressed ideas on the importance of culture in the accompanying graphic. We could expand his thought by just saying that culture is the heartbeat of the school. It's what keeps everything going; it's what keeps people excited about the process. It is what you see and feel when you walk in the door. It's the way adults interact, the way adults interact with children, the way the children communicate with each other. It's the way the leadership interacts with the staff, whether it's the teachers or the custodial staff or the support people or even outside partnerships. Culture is the way you create a family within a school building. If it's a team of people who are attacking a challenge, then typically you have more success at it.

I've already told you what the culture was at Shabazz in those days. It was one sentence, a core belief that was the exact opposite of what a lofty mission statement. It was "This is Shabazz High School. It is what it is." Teachers said it, students said it. One day there was a fire drill. When it was over, we had to check all of the students into the building, so they didn't bring any weapons in. A young man came to the door, and a teacher asked him to stop.

"You have to wait," the teacher said, "or you're going to get suspended."

The student replied, "Man, this is Shabazz. You're not going to do anything." And he pushed past the teacher and into the school.

That's what needed fixing. Students had to have belief in the system that we established. They wanted to
have faith in the teachers. Teachers had to trust in the
leadership, that he/she would lead the way everyone
expected. Teachers had to buy into a mindset that children, whether at-risk or not at-risk, could learn just the
same. They had to begin believing in themselves. They
had to start to understand how to interact with a challenging student, that the answer wasn't always just to
suspend the student. We had to start thinking about restorative practice, ways in which we could have a conversation around what happened and better ways to
deal with it, aside from supporting this whole school-
to-prison pipeline epidemic that has been taking place
in urban schools.

The American Civil Liberties Union (ACLU) describes
the school-to-prison pipeline as "a disturbing national trend wherein children are funneled out of public
schools and into the juvenile and criminal justice systems. Many of these children have learning disabilities
or histories of poverty, abuse, or neglect, and would
benefit from additional educational and counseling services. Instead, they are isolated, punished, and pushed
out." The ACLU goes on to say, "Students of color are
especially vulnerable to push-out trends and the dis-
criminatory application of discipline."

The Center for Disease Control speaks directly to the
history of violence of children and adults growing up
in urban areas who have committed crimes from murder to robbery to molestations. The CDC deemed this

history of violence a public health issue. It's a condition, and things must be done to undo all of the things that people have accepted to be the norm. You can just imagine, and this is a worst-case scenario, but I've watched it affect some of the best kids as well.

There was a young man named Al-Tamar and his mom. Dad was in jail, a gang member, as was his mom. So naturally, the son embraced gang culture. He was not an official gang member; he was an athlete. The young man left his neighborhood on the south side of Newark and attended East Side High School to play sports. However, he just couldn't get it right there, no matter how good he was. He just couldn't get it together in the climate, and he ended up in Shabazz. Meanwhile, I left East Side high school also and had gone on to become the chairperson of mathematics at Shabazz. We were reunited because he was my student at Eastside. This young man was an exceptional athlete, but every day he went home and interacted with gang culture. He experienced the neighborhood block where people sell drugs to make money. He encountered the glorification of your neighborhood drug dealer who had all of the women, all of the clothes, all of the cars. Al-Tamar idolized that person. So when he went to school, he behaved like that person, gaining popularity and becoming an icon himself in the schoolhouse.

Gang culture has become a mainstream thing amongst hip-hop enthusiasts, and I'm an avid hip-hop listener. A lot of the slang, the terminology created for them to communicate, is now something you can withing hear your latest hip-hop song. The idea of wearing a bandana is more like a fad than it is a representation of a group of people you associate with a gang. It's become cool to be a part of a gang. Why would this be a typical thing? Why would that be acceptable? Why would anybody not say that this not ok? What's happening? Nevertheless, many of our students live this and learn that it is okay to look the other way to violence or be labeled a snitch. Not snitching is the thing you're supposed to do. Though you know your next door neighbor has a gun, and he's a murderer you're not supposed to tell the police. These become foundational principles for the living or should I say surviving. You can imagine the beauty of what we were building at Shabazz. We understood what the children faced and had every intent to undo all of it.

I've mentioned that in observing things around the school and imagining myself as the principal, I'd developed a 90-day plan. Now that the job was mine, I had to start bringing it to life. Football, which had helped me so much in my days as a Paterson high school student, was going to play a huge role in the Turnaround at Shabazz.

It began with a very detailed game plan, followed by formation of a team. It would be my player draft. What would Day 1 through 90 look like at the new Shabazz? Then, whom should do this work? Who would support the people doing the job? What types of partnerships did I need to put in place to address the things that we lacked? I did not have the bandwidth to do it all.

Fresh in my mind was the essential question in the interview, the one about the way I communicate. In putting together a game plan, I needed to read more educationally sound, empirical research to develop my global understanding of the language of the pedagogue. It was imperative that I approached the new job with the utmost clarity. I had to convey what we planned to do, and how, and why. And I needed people who would be receptive to ideas. It would be the Shabazz Turnaround team. My immediate task was to contact everybody whom I had envisioned on the staff and move them where they needed to be.

Faheem Ellis was a physical education teacher who dealt with a large number of students and got them to do what he needed them to do in class. He was also a coach. Faheem was also an athlete. He happened to be the athletic director at Shabazz and enjoyed great success. He did great work for our girl's basketball team in hiring the right coach. He was even responsible for bringing in Coach Darnell Grant, who was the head football coach as well as our Dean of Discipline. So Faheem understood it. He knew what people to pick, and he knew how to use them to maximize their potential. So I thought if I can get this guy to be my vice principal in charge of climate and culture, we would have success.

I would contemplate on a regular basis, and I knew if I was leaving the scheduling position, who would that person be? Who would fill my shoes as a Master Scheduler? I needed a person with a math mind, who'd be way more meticulous than I had ever been with the data and the spreadsheets. Shabazz needed someone who knew what students need and knew the things you must move to create 20 opportunities versus having something in one place that minimizes the chances for student course selection. We had someone like that on our team. Her name was Ms. Baskerville, and we weren't maximizing her talents. She was the 12th-grade administrator doing senior class advisor stuff, such as testing. This woman was a phenomenal chairperson of mathematics. She is detailed to a fault.

I embraced the fact that her meticulous behavior around spreadsheets and students and not leaving any stone unturned was what we needed. Ms. Baskerville would maximize the opportunity for students, as well as for staff members who were adamant about having a schedule in their classroom to just improve their level of dedication because there were some things they wanted. At the time, there was a sense she was leaving us. Ms. Baskerville was transitioning back to a demotion as a math chairperson at West Side High School. And she was satisfied with it, as there were things she wanted to do such as starting a family. She was willing to take the lesser role to do more in her personal life. I was able to convince her to get on board with us and promised that I would honor her family responsibili-ties by providing her with additional support.

My third person to lead the instruction needed to be someone I could trust, someone I knew would never sugarcoat what the situation was. This person needed to be someone who, if I left him or her to do a job, they would be amazing at it, because their dedication to children was equal to mine. That person was Allison DeVaughn, the English chairperson.

Even if you have the right people on your team, you have to be clear and make your case. One of the very, very important things I understood about educators was they don't want to just take your word for it. When they see someone new to a position, there's doubt in their minds. They had experienced a ton of pain and uncertainty with previous principals. They had heard false promises. As the leader, I needed to have something that supported my way of thinking. One of the things that aligned perfectly with my beliefs was Dr. Wayne K. Hoy's theory of academic optimism. It gave us a roadmap for the flow of change. It would guide and propel student growth from a dismal place of failure to a newfound sense of academic success.

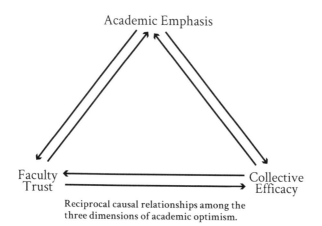

Reciprocal causal relationships among the three dimensions of academic optimism.

Hoy uses a triangular approach, with three ideas working in tandem. First was **collective efficacy**, which meant that teachers believed in themselves and in their capacity to do what was necessary for the job. To be aboard the bus to do the job, you have to have trust in yourself, trust that you can come to work every day and reach children and bring them from where they are to where they need to be.

The second part of the triangle is **faculty trust**. The difference between collective efficacy and faculty trust is that faculty trust is not a trust in self or other teachers. It was trust in the students: Do you believe that the children can meet the bar that you are going to set? Or are you going into the game saying to yourself, "These kids can't do it; thus I want to dumb down what I'm teaching them.?" Doing so will ensure that the students will achieve only to that level.

The last piece of academic optimism is the educational **emphasis**. It's straightforward. Are the teachers doing the work? There are a ton of factors or variables that go into this success process. If we did not have a strong focus on planning and delivering excellent lessons for children on a regular basis, you could guarantee failure. Students spend most of their school day inside a classroom. If it's an eight-hour day, that student is spending six-and-a-half hours in front of a teacher. Those teachers need to anticipate what students may not understand long before one of them asks what something means.

You see in the diagram that on each leg of the triangle, the arrows go both ways. That's because all these elements — trusting yourself, trusting in the students' ability to get it done, and putting forth the effort day in and day out — are working in tandem. They are not separate pieces. Our plan was not a situation where we build collective efficacy and then build faculty trust. These things should happen at the same time. They need to be in motion at the same time. To do them separately would only prolong the success process or the closing of the achievement gap. It's a perfect pyramid of success, as Hoy described it.

Core beliefs (see diagram) are what everyone can look for and be grounded. Take faculty trust in the students. What is it that you believe students can and cannot do in the building? Posting these core beliefs in every classroom is helpful. If students and staff receive a message on a regular basis and that information is discussed the core values become a part of you and part of the school's culture. We become the way we behave because of our beliefs. It's not unlike a religion. There are staples within a religion, whether you hold faithful to Christianity, or to Islam or anything else. You act a certain way because this is something you believe. The core beliefs are a way of being inside this building when thinking about students.

Initially, I adopted our core beliefs from Mike Miles. He was in Colorado at the time but also doing lots of work in New Jersey. I had many sessions with him, as well as with several other educators in New Jersey. I agreed with the core beliefs he was promoting as a superintendent in a district in Colorado. He had astonishing results.

My idea was to put Hoy's theory together with Miles' core beliefs. Aligning the core beliefs with the academic optimism theory could make a point to the staff: Here's something that's happening in real life, in real situations. People are doing it and getting results. Dr.

CORE BELIEFS
MALCOLM X SHABAZZ HIGH SCHOOL

Inspiration: We believe that by inspiring our students we can instill the desire to achieve greatness.

Motivation: Sports and career pathways, internships, and career opportunities will provide the incentive to motivate our students to persevere and succeed.

Purpose: We believe that our purpose is to provide the resources that will lead our students to successful outcomes.

Accountability: We hold each other and ourselves to the highest standards of excellence.

Commitment: We are committed to creating a supportive school environment that's inclusive of students, community, and staff

Transformation: We believe in providing a pathway to transition our students to college and life through life-changing experiences.

Hoy has conducted 20 years of research on how we optimize for academic success. Marrying Hoy's theory and Miles' core beliefs would yield the success we were looking for, and we would have a chance later on to develop our own, which we did.

During crunch time, with six days to open the school, you make a choice. It was a leap of faith grounded in strong beliefs. But a leap of faith nevertheless.

With more than ten years worth of research available for me to analyze, I made a firm prediction about the results. I wanted to be informed. I couldn't just accept Miles' core beliefs without knowing that there was empirical research behind them. When I found alignment between Dr. Hoy's theory and Mike Miles core beliefs, I knew it was the thing to choose to get us going.

In introducing this alignment to the staff, I had to present my depth of knowledge and explain how I arrived at this point. Again, with the damage done at the school, it wasn't going to be okay just to say, "Here's where we're going, follow me." I had to go through the pro-cess with them, how I understood academic optimism and the way it aligned with the core beliefs selected. Then I had to create a space in which they could real-ize that this was a start. The message was this: We're in the thick of things right now. You're just returning to school and students will be here in two days. Let's understand that we will create our system to foster our own culture that is unique to Shabazz in a year's time. However, we can't enter the school without something that bonds us, that guides us on how we feel about ourselves and the students we serve.

I posted the core beliefs on the smart board, went through the process, presented it, took questions, let people express their thoughts on it so that we could have clarity. Every teacher was then mandated to post our core beliefs in their classroom.

As the challenges to turn around Shabazz persisted, I read many more books and became heavily influenced by the work of Lee Bolman and Terrence Deal, who wrote the best-selling book "Reframing Organizations: Artistry, Choice, and Leadership.

Published in 1984, the bookoutlines four frames, or lenses, through which people can view the world: structural, political, human resource and symbolic. You can see from the diagram what each frame addresses.

With the children soon to be walking through the door, Shabazz had goals, some fundamental beliefs, and a plan for going forward. But we would need tools to make the theory and the plan work. That brought us to something I call "Levers." We needed specific actions or thoughts that, when exercised, could produce dramatic effects. We wanted to identify key areas we could hone in on and be very particular about the functionality of each "Lever." Notice the key phrase in that sentence — "be very particular." Many people identify vital areas when they begin a project. Then other urgent matters appear, and the essential areas identified get lost.

FOUR-FRAME MODEL OVERVIEW

	STRUCTURAL	HUMAN RESOURCES	POLITICAL	SYMBOLIC
Metaphor for Organization	Factory/Machine	Family	Jungle	Carnival, temple, theatre
Central Concepts	Rules, roles, goals, policies, technology, environment	Needs, skills, relationships	Power, conflict, competition, organisational policies	Culture, meaning, metaphor, ritual, ceremony, stories, heroes
Image of Leadership	Social architecture	Empowerment	Advocacy	Inspiration
Leadership Challenge	Attune structure to task, technology, environment	Align organizational and human needs	Develop agenda and power base	Create faith, beauty, meaning
Organizational Ethic	Excellence	Carin	Justice	Faith
Leadership Contribution	Authorship	Love	Power	Significance

Without constant attention and follow-through, even the best of ideas fail. A constant focus on "Levers" will help you mitigate failed ideas.

To understand what these educational "Levers" are, picture a dam. There's a lever that controls a gate. When we position the lever one way, the gates hold the water. When there's a shift in the lever, the gates let the water out, creating massive change on the other side. It can irrigate crops, or produce waterways. That's what our "Levers" at Shabazz were all about; they embody the concept of pieces of equipment that allow you to make maximum changes with minimal effort.

10 LEVER 1
MINDSET

MINDSET

From the outset, we talked changing the Shabazz mindset. There was a horrible level of belief in the possibilities for our school. I had to attack that and mindset was the best way to do it. As a "Lever," mindset affected teacher morale, student attendance, and teacher attendance. All of those things changed because of a transformation in the staff and students mindset.

It all began with a change in how we looked at things. "Mindset," a book by Carol Dweck, put down on paper some things that would have an immense impact on Shabazz.

Early in the book, Dweck quotes 19th-century French

psychologist Alfred Binet, inventor of the IQ test. Dweck cites Binet's book "Modern Ideas About Children," which says, "A few modern philosophers ... assert that an individual's intelligence is a fixed quantity which cannot increase. We must protest and react against this brutal pessimism with practice, training, and above all, method; we manage to increase our attention, our memory, our judgment and literally to become more intelligent than we were before."

What resonated with me was how Dweck expanded and developed Binet's ideas. She spoke of the fixed mindset versus the growth mindset. When describing a fixed mindset, Dweck was talking about a person who is not open, who have experienced so much failure that they cannot produce any more or don't believe that they can produce at all. On the other hand, a person with a growth mindset lives and works with the belief that things can change, that individuals can make changes in their lives and in their thinking that will open up a world of success.

When I read "Mindset," I felt this concept was what Shabazz needed to understand for us to begin moving in the right direction. Because at Shabazz we had to overcome the mindset that nothing would ever solve the problems. I've already told you that people would say, "This is Shabazz. It is what it is." Meaning that if a fight broke out, "It is what it is." If kids smoked marijuana in the hallways, "It is what it is." If young people were caught having sex, "It is what it is." If we had to go out on five fire drills a day, "It is what it is." Everyone had this fixed belief that it could never change. Shabazz had to change the idea that nothing could change.

It's very accurate that children come from a place — sometimes, not all the time — where they believe that the craziest situations are common. They've gone through experiences that would seem intolerable to any traditional living human or a citizen of America. These encounters were acceptable in the world in which many of our children lived. Just like it was for me in Paterson. I understood why the students at Shabazz would think that the status quo was okay, just based on my experiences. Our students were looking for someone to take an interest in them and then keep their promise and not lack integrity about things they were saying they were going to do. The students could smell a fake a mile away. If anyone were to have success in changing students mindsets, they needed first to understand that you understood them. And I was that guy.

I hired people who added value to that conversation, so I didn't always need to be the person in front of the student. I identified people who would work in the school, who could have conversations about students life experiences. You could think of this hiring process as a football draft. You pick the person you believe can help the most in a critical area. We couldn't afford any bad draft picks.

In "Making Hope Happen: Create the Future You Want," Dr. Shane Lopez opens with a story about a sick veteran whose kidney disease left him without hope of saving his farm. This man, whose name was John, had even threatened to kill himself. "John had lost his way," Lopez wrote. He wasn't getting from Point A to Point B, and "He needed new strategies for getting to his old goals, or he needed a new Point B." Long story short, John made it. Lopez writes on page 11, "Although some people still believe that hope is too "soft" to be studied scientifically, other researchers and I have convincing evidence that hopeful thought and behavior propel everyone toward well-being and success." Lopez goes on to say, "while only half the population measures high in hope, hope can be learned, and the hopeful among us can play a powerful role in spreading hope to others."

And even though I may have believed that intuitively, the reading of Dweck, the reading of Angela Duckworth's "Grit," and the reading of Lopez showed me that there were compelling ideas and relevant science that we could use.

Peter Senge, a systems scientist, talks about mental models. People form mental models about the world from the way they grow up and the things that they experience, which is what, sometimes, creates disconnects between adults. Humans grow up in these paths and develop their own beliefs, yet are expected to come together for one purpose. A pathway dichotomy of multiple adults is extremely difficult to navigate. When this exists, what you say does not matter much, because each person perceives the world differently from another. How do you fix that? You've got to get those people to believe in the same thing. For us, we had to develop the belief that we could turn Shabazz around. To do so, I needed to identify something that everyone was emotionally attached to, which was the fear of Shabazz closing forever. I wanted to instill fear. I wanted them to feel that not agreeing that this is possible will result in more cuts to the staff, more turmoil in the building and unsafe conditions, the possibility of a charter school takeover, or school closure. Let's be real. We were losing students like blood squirting out of a major artery. We went from 1,500 to 500 students in less than four years.

Students can see through the fluff in people, and what they claim to be or perpetuate. And I refused to be anything other than what I told them I would be. I've always been me. I've never been a yeller, a screamer, or disrespectful. I treated staff and students with respect. And in our conversations, no matter if they were wrong or right, I always did the ethical thing. I never asked myself "Is he/she going to side with me because they are my friend?" or "Is he/she going to do something bad to me because he/she doesn't like me?" It was always about right and wrong no matter who you were.

I can recall conversations with students who were getting suspended, it went like this: "The policy is if you fight you get three days suspension. This decision has nothing to do with me hating you or loving you. Did you fight?"

"Yeah."

"What does it say should happen?"

"Oh, I should get three days."

"That's why you're getting suspended because you fought. But I do love you, and I show you in every way, shape, form and fashion, the way I support you, the places I show up at, the things I help with, and the way I work with your family. The stuff that I'll do just to make sure you have what you need to be successful. Along with everybody else. But what I won't do is compromise that because I want you to like me. I will not comprise that."

They respected the fact that I wouldn't compromise what was right because of a relationship. It got around the school that "Mills don't play that. If he says he's going to do it, he's going to do it. So, respect him and understand that's what you're going to get." That turned a lot of things around. Kids would say, "We don't fight at Shabazz out of respect for me. Don't bring that stuff to school. He's obviously trying to do something right for us, so we don't want to bring negativity to the building." That's not to say we never had fights. That would be false. But that year we went from 139 to 52. That's a tremendous decrease in one school year with a set of students who were said to be the most at-risk in Newark, based on budgetary calculations.

A mindset shift could not happen without buy-in from the staff. Once you have the mindset, it is important to find others who have a similar mindset and are willing to follow a strong leader. It's time for the staff draft. Your team is one of the most critical assets of your school, but putting that team together can be a tiring process.

If the school is new, then it's only about locating successful individuals, interviewing them, and ensuring that they understand your goals and process. If you are taking over the reins of an established school, then you need to assess your staff and be prepared to make changes seriously.

Someone needed to come forward. And someone did. It was after I presented the opening day presentation to the entire staff about what I intended to do, the things that were going on around us, the variables that were affecting us, and everybody knows that this is it. Either we get it right, or you go home, which meant that someone was going to foreclose on the house. We called Shabazz the doghouse. I said, "You can have your own home, or we can share it. At the doghouse. That meant that a charter school would lease our space, or we were going to have to share space with another district school, with multiple principals. Then you will deal with another dynamic thereby creating additional roadblocks and hindering progress.

I was wrapping up the PowerPoint and walking over to get my flash drive out of my computer when a man named Darnell Grant, everyone called him Coach Grant, approached me. He was the SOS teacher. That means Suspension Off-Site. It's the SOS teacher who deals with all of the things that no one else wants to take on. Coach Grant is a person who gets every problematic student pushed into their room, and is expected to organize or create some learning. There are random grades of boys and girls who have done the worst of the worst in class and needed to be on timeout. He knew as well as anyone the depth and scope of problems at Shabazz. And there was something else about Coach Grant. He was also the head football coach. I told you earlier how important football was to me during my high school years. It was about to become important once again.

"Mills, I want to talk to you."

Coach Grant got my attention. Grant had an immense influence on his players. No one knew it at the time, but he would be named New Jersey football Coach of the Year in 2014 when he led our Bulldogs to a state championship. This feat, coming one year after the team suffered a last-second loss, was about more than football, according to Grant.

"For the kids to not give up and not stop fighting and to not stop believing in the system and doing things the right way and treating people the right way, you can't stop smiling thinking about it," Grant said.

Grant has a degree in political science, so he's always strategizing and thinking about things. I guess the spark went off in his head that, "Hey, I can work with this leader and we can do some amazing things."

I said, "What's up, coach?"

What he said next was music to my ears. He said, "We can do some big things with the football team and this whole thing about mindset because the students are ecstatic about you. They believe in you. I want you to come talk to them and create dialogue, talk to them about what you need from them and I want to support that."

That was quite a speech, and it meant a lot to me. Coach Grant knew something about quick turnarounds. In the four seasons, before he arrived at Shabazz, the team won only seven games while losing 40. That changed immediately. Grant got the attention and respect of the players. When he speaks in the pre-game huddle, the players are silent except for the two words that they shout: "Yes, sir!"

The concept of me approaching the football team was this idea that you could get more out of children who connect with their passion and purpose. Football players will endure excruciating pain because they are passionate about something. Their enthusiasm is why they all came together. They had a mission. Every football player, whether 5-foot-2 or 6-foot-8, believed their purpose was to become a professional football player. I understood that concept long before I knew the research. If I could identify students who connect to something that's greater than school, then I could motivate them to do something about their environment and set the example for other students in the building.

When you have control of the football team, which are the biggest and mightiest bodies in the building, it is more probable that other students will fall in line. Coach Grant had the respect of 80 football players on a daily basis.

We began approaching and improving the school the way a coach would handle a sports program. The teachers would function like assistant coaches, and of course, the students would be like players. The news site nj.com did a documentary on our efforts, titled "Saving Shabazz: The long-shot battle to transform a failing school."

Selling a new mindset wasn't always easy. Some people were not buying into the concept. We had a teacher named Mr. Poll, and the whole mindset shift was not happening for him. He would have a ton of disciplinary infraction problems. No matter what we did, no matter how many conferences we set up for him he wouldn't embrace the changes occurring at Shabazz. It was important to me that all teachers felt powerful and confident to enforce rules in their classroom. Teachers who shifted their mindset would say, "I have power here, I have a say in what happens, students get what they're supposed to get," Mr. Poll wasn't feeling it. He had been rated ineffective. A few times he had been rated partially effective, and he would write lengthy re-buttals to say that all the things observed weren't happening. The funny thing was that despite his lack of belief and conspiracy theory about what was occurring, there were many improvements and the central office administration recognized our progress. He would tell people, "Mr. Mills needs to stop doing all that work because they're using him. They're going to fire him just like they fired all the other ones. It's just a matter of time. He's not safe." That's what he would perpetuate around the building. Other teachers would just say, "But guess what? The test scores went up. Students are graduating at higher rates. And my students aren't bad anymore. If I tell them that a student needs to intervention, I need a parent conference, it happens. So I'm not sure what your issues are."

I began to see the mindset shift in November or December. Initially, it was just a facade. Every teacher would say, "You're doing good, Mr. Mills, keep it up." What that meant was the students did not acclimate to the new changes yet, so they were not acting out of control. People would say that the first month was always normal, where students are trying to get accustomed to the systems and how they can get around them. People figured that when we got to October, pandemonium would begin again. Students would start fighting, students would be disrespectful, and the administration would lose control of the building. When we made it through the second month, and there was no fire alarm pulls, and students were held accountable for things they were doing, there was a feeling of progress. Hallways were clear, security guards were working to get that done, custodial workers were telling students that they needed to be in class, lunch ladies had a voice, and everybody who had eyes. Every adult in the building had a say in what should and shouldn't happen. By the time November came, and we had no fire alarm pulls and a small number of suspensions, I began to see and hear from staff, "I want to help. What can I do? I can do more. And you saw a change in teacher attendance. Teachers started coming to work more. They weren't taking off as much. And they weren't afraid to speak up. That was a massive turnaround in itself. I swear, in previous years the students instilled so much fear into the teachers that they would not tell when they were doing the wrong thing.

I saw a change in teachers. Just two years ago a teacher said, "I don't want any problems, but I saw him punch the girl in the face. But I don't want anything to happen to me." Now teachers say, "This is the one, Mr. Mills. I saw it." That's when I knew the mindset had changed. They began to believe that I would support them and ensure that any person, staff or student, would be held accountable for inappropriate behavior.

Once our new mindset got through to the teachers and students, exciting possibilities began to show themselves. Dweck says in Mindset, "as you begin to understand the fixed and growth mindsets, you will see how one thing leads to another ..." In our case, our growth mindset led to increased commitment, actions and results. The turnaround had begun in earnest.

11 LEVER 2 STRUCTURE

STRUCTURE

The kids were out of control. But I felt if we could only organize correctly, we could cut down on the number of disciplinary infractions we were having. A simple thing like changing the way the kids entered the building made a difference. Reducing the number of open doors meant we didn't have to duplicate resources. We no longer had to have security guards at every corner of the building. We would place more guards in more strategic locations.

We created new structures at Shabazz in a variety of ways. One had to do with the physical building. Another changed the configuration of the administration cabinet. Initially, and throughout high schools in

America, there is an administrative cabinet structure that is very hierarchical (See graphic). Rising through the ranks as an administrator your colleagues pull you in multiple directions, it makes it difficult to be successful at one thing powerfully. As a chairperson, I was not only responsible for the math teachers and evaluating them. I also needed to deal with the disciplinary infractions of the students, their parents, and the list goes on. As a vice-principal, I had to facilitate the entire 11th grade, and all that it entailed: testing, parents, infractions, fights, observations, as well as build the master schedule. I had to change teachers and student schedules as well as ensure that teachers were in the right places when students arrived for class.

Old Shabazz Structure

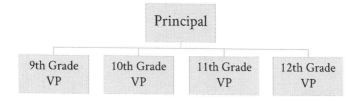

I needed to fix that. I needed to create a way to improve the critical functions within the school. The administrators are required to do many things, yet I need them to focus on a specific goal to improve student achievement. Grade levels are traditional. Administrators in charge of entire grade levels have too cumbersome of a task. You're honestly running your very own school. I didn't see the regular structure as plausible, so I shifted it to create the triangle (See diagram). You can see in the picture that, unlike the academic optimism depiction, there are no reverse arrows. Each of these three administrators interfaces entirely with me, touching the others only at a single point. At the center of the triangle is the principal. Then there are three arms, one apiece on each side of the triangle. Instead of assigning a grade-level principal to do everything, we identified three things that are vital to success. One is student achievement, another is the climate and the culture, and the third is student support services and scheduling. I told the administrators that they would no longer be in charge of a grade level. In place of the grade-level principals, there would be three people in charge of the three vital areas within the building.

New Shabazz Structure

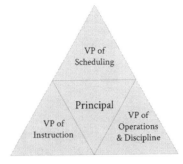

Though all three were necessary climate and culture was an essential part of turning around the school in year one. The bulk of this chapter will focus on environment and culture. However, I discuss the other two legs in Chapters 13 to 16. The structure is a prerequisite for the success of the model; if you have a weak structure, you're probably going to have an uncertain climate and culture. You have to build out the structure to maximize the potential for cultivating an atmosphere in which students want to be in school and are excited to attend. As this is happening and students are following rules, simultaneously you ensure that you are providing the same type of focus to academic rigor and teacher quality. If these two things aren't happening, ultimately you will lose. You can have a very quiet school and have poor performing teachers and students. Also, you can have remarkable educators where students don't walk into class to experience their awesomeness because the climate and culture are poor—where students think it's okay to treat the school like a mall or like a social experience rather than a place to become empowered.

Thus, I reconfigured my administrative cabinet in a three-pronged approach to address the things I thought were extremely important to the success of the school. One was about climate and culture, another was student achievement, and the third was student support services. People made the argument that if you have a great instructional program, then discipline and culture and climate will fix itself. But I found that one without the other results in failure. I watched that occur three times with three different principals; they had chosen one and not the other. Thus I had to do these things simultaneously if the turnaround was going to happen fast. I picked an administrator whom I thought had all the attributes of a structuralist who could deliver on a daily basis on ensuring that people did what they were asked to do. I told him he would never, ever enter a classroom. Your only responsibility is to guarantee that these hallways are empty during instructional time, that people are doing the job that they've been assigned to do, and students were where they're supposed to be consistent from 8:10 in the morning to 3:31 every day. Then I built a team around him.

This person was Faheem Ellis, who I had promoted from athletic director to Vice Principal in charge of climate and culture. I thought he would do a fantastic job only because he understood complex systems and how to maximize staff output within them. If a teacher had an issue with a student, they could quickly remove the problem by sending him/her to a place where we contact parents, set up a parent conference and got communicated to the teacher, who will facilitate the meeting the next day. We also incorporated technology to help mitigate our climate and culture issues by purchasing a web-based discipline program called "On Course." This program changed the game! It allowed the classroom teacher to report a behavioral infraction from anywhere in the school building. Moreover, once the teacher hit "enter," my cell phone and those on the climate and culture team were notified of the infraction, what happened, who the student was, and the location of the incident. "On Course" improved the lines of communication for the entire administrative team. We no longer needed to debrief about climate and culture at the end of each day because the system sent this information out to the whole staff before the end of each school day.

Technology caused a lot of havoc as well when it was used to destroy the climate and culture we were building. Students were bringing cell phones in, and the phones would be the topic of discussion in every classroom. The cell phones were the very thing that would bring outsiders to the building with misinformation about what was occurring inside. For example, a child brought his cellphone into school. He started arguing with another young man, and they begin fighting. One young man got the best of the other, and the student that lost the battle ran away and took to his cellphone with him. A few members of the young man family happened to be involved in a gang, and he reached out to them and told them, "Come to the school right now. I just got jumped." He was describing to his family that 12 people jumped him and they'd threatened to kill him after school. We went outside after school that they and saw carloads of gang members looking to harm a 15-year-old student because of hear-say, which was false. So I knew we could not have cell phones in school. I thought it would be hard to do; I went and found cell phone lockers and bought all this stuff to try to make students feel comfortable about giving me their cell phones. The idea was to print the pupil's picture along with their grade level and ID number on a Ziploc bag. Students were required to put their cell phone in it when they walked into school, and they would get it back at the end of the day. Who would have thought that students would have bought into that? Well, it worked, and they did!

Collecting cell phones at the beginning of the day did two things. First, it reduced the number of students who wanted to bring a cell phone to school. They thought, "I'm not giving you my cell phone." But we made it clear and I also aligned it with school policy. Some people might argue, "That's not your property. You don't want to be responsible for it." But what the policy says, at least at Newark public schools, is that a child cannot have a phone that has a camera or can take pictures. Not many cell phones get created without the ability to take a picture. So guess what? Students can't bring their phones into the building. However, we did them a favor by securing it and ensuring they got it back after school. The cell phone collection strategy eliminated the back and forth between the classroom teachers, who were fighting against every social media outlet in the country. It was a case of, "here I'm trying to teach you trigonometry but Facebook has the funniest videos ever, or Instagram has everything that's going on in someone else's class."

Competing with a cell phone is difficult. Therefore we eliminated the issue. Also, this strategy stopped communication with people outside the school whom we didn't want to get incorrect information before the administration gave them the correct narrative. So if a student fought with another student, they needed to make a phone call on the landline instead of being able to readily text friends, family, and associates to come to the school building. The administrative team was now able to get the right narrative to parents and parents arrived at the school either to get their child or to have a parent conference. Amazing! One of the best things we ever did.

We were taking large-scale issues that were just so frequent that you couldn't control it, and reducing it to nothing because of the consistency in our structures. Whether or not I talk to the vice-principals in the morning, they had a printout of any child who got in trouble. They could click a box, and another report opens up explaining what they got in trouble for, and what reprimand they received. Also, we were able to communicate this information from the discipline office back to the teacher's computer each day. So they would know that on this date a parent conference would be happening and they should be present. I knew what was going on and could contact any of my administrators to see if things were okay. "On Course" also created a way for us to be proactive. No different than the data we collected on teachers and building their quality, we collected data on students and their most frequent infractions and which grade levels had the most infractions. For example, we could see that the ninth-graders had the most instances of disrespect to teachers. The administrative team pulled together, "Okay, we need to create a proactive program for the freshman on how to interact with adults." The data revealed that the 11th-grade students had had the most fights in November. We could go deeper. Let's see; there were ten fights. But was it ten fights with one student involved in all of them? We could pinpoint and see that something is going on with a student. We would troubleshoot that and eliminate problems.

Then there's the matter of social media. You wouldn't imagine how powerful it is. Students don't treat social media the way adults do; most adults will say, "You got to be careful what you put up there. You're leaving your mark on the world. People are watching it, and it never goes away." Most adults probably 30 and up are very conscious of what they post. Teenage children act as if it's reality TV. They want the world to know. Imagine being a high school student, being popular, and then every student in the school follows you on Twitter. Everything you Tweet, everyone knows. You're the reality TV star of the high school. What I understood was I didn't have access to every child, but they needed to have access to me because if they have access to me, we could reduce the number of issues as well as collect ideas from the students. We could take the best of these ideas and implement them in the school so students could feel connected to the culture. So I created a Twitter and Instagram account, @principalmills. On the back of every ID that got issued in the school was my handle for Twitter. Students would reach out for a myriad of reasons. The best one was a young lady who said, "I want you to know that tomorrow I'm going to fight at the school." I replied, "Please send me your mom's number." I called the mother and asked her what was going on. She said, "This girl has been saying things to her, and we're just tired of that family, so I told her if she gets in your face again, you need to go ahead and handle it."

Now I had to troubleshoot this situation with an adult who's telling her daughter to go to school and fight. Advising your child to fight is not an okay. We encouraged students to have conversations and dialogue before they ever resort to fisticuffs. I told her, "Here's what I need you to do. Bring your daughter to school tomorrow. I'm going to reach out to the other parent. I have access to her via the Web, and we'll set up a parent conference so we can resolve the matter." The following day both parents came with their children. We had a conversation with the young lady. It turns out the young lady who claimed harassment was angering the other young lady with friends at the bus stop near the school. Thankfully, we were able to get to the bottom of it. I swear to you, six times out of ten, the families are connected to each other somehow. One of the parents will say, "Aren't you such and such? Aren't you married to my cousin?" That's what happened here, and the woman said to her daughter, "Girl, that's family. Why are you acting like this?" They shook hands, hugged, we ended the meeting, and what I require all children to do when leaving any of our restorative conferences is to apologize to each other. I will say, "Get up. You want to be an adult; you have to behave like an adult. You must mend things like an adult. You must look her/him in the eye and apologize to each other before you leave the conference." When parents are present, this is easier to accomplish. As much as people might argue that parents aren't involved in high schoolers lives, their children respect them. When you can get them inside of the building, you'll see a different child. And when they know how the parent values the administrator, you get a different student. That was a significant key to our success.

The other part of Twitter that was useful is its database of text messages that are character-searchable. If you put a keyword on Twitter, you can identify a lot. I had students following me because they wanted to communicate, and I would retweet them. But I would craft searches on Twitter such as "Shabazz High School." I would search "Shabazz fights." I would search "Shabazz Mills." Just to see if things would come up based on what was happening with the students. I was able to troubleshoot tons of things that were brewing in the community with searches on my Twitter account. For example, I searched "Shabazz fights," and what comes up? "It's going down at Shabazz tomorrow. We're going to f@$* those girls up." So I put out a Tweet, "For all of you who are following me, and for those who are planning a fight at Shabazz tomorrow, there will be none! And you probably won't be attending this school anymore if something should occur." I contacted my administrators in charge of climate, and culture and we were able to address this at morning convocation, which was held daily for the first 20 minutes of each school day.

One day I was at the Essex County scholar dinner. My valedictorian and my salutatorian were receiving awards. While there I got a text message that there was a shooting at the corner of West Bigelow and Johnson. That's the corner where everyone enters the campus near the gym. Sal, one of our students, a magnificent athlete, and a leader, was a guy who had everything. He was 6-foot-4, 190 pounds, a charming student and extremely popular. By default, Sal was the leader in everything. So he had enemies, and they attempted to gun him down right on the corner, immediately after his conversation with the recruitment coach from Miami. I went on Twitter and started pulling up searches. What did I find? A young man who was with Sal tweeting, "If you're going to dump on us, don't close your eyes." That's slang for, "If you're going to shoot at us, don't close your eyes while you're doing it. Look and see where you're shooting." It was like reality TV. The young man had just finished a shooting outside of Shabazz High School, one of his friends got arrested, and the others were taken in for questioning. The young man posted his thoughts on Twitter for all his friends to see, taunting the people who had shot at him. That's what I found through a Twitter search. Though all searches are not this intense, I would encourage all educators to conduct random twitter searches and see if what you find can lead to mitigation of issues within the lives of students in your schools.

Another aspect of structure my team and I addressed was the schedule. The schedule is the foundation of it all. What footsteps are the students taking in and around the building? How do you create a way for the most novice person to navigate the school building? In our schedule, we put the entire freshman class on the fourth floor. If you were a sophomore, you were on the third floor, old building. A junior, second floor, old building. If you were a senior, you were on the second floor, new building. In their class schedule, for their primary core courses, we made the footsteps a minute apart from each other. If your English class were room 222, then your math class would be room 223, and your history class would be room 224.

We needed to create the opportunity for students to get the things they needed to graduate. Sometimes schedules where designed where you can't take algebra and geometry because the rooms don't work, the time frames don't work, the teacher's schedule conflicted, and it was imperative to me as a former master scheduler that this didn't occur. We were able to make that happen, so instead of having a student take filler courses, they were able to take the classes they needed to meet graduation requirements.

We changed the classroom sessions from blocks to periods. Block scheduling put students in class for a longer duration, and some studies say the more time they can spend in a specific location, the higher their level of retention. However, because our teachers had not been trained in the block appropriately, it didn't increase retention. Teachers would slow down a 45-minute lesson to go for 80 minutes instead of teaching more. There were also facilitation issues. Teachers weren't able to adequately plan for 80 minutes to keep the student engaged. A quick fix for a better learning style until we could deliver more professional development was to go to a period schedule, which took our blocks from 84 minutes to 42 minutes. This created space within the school day to let our students get on the same page before they went to class each morning, which was huge! The entire school building went into the gymnasium every morning. Students got to speak to me, to see me, and I got to lead them in a discussion. We began with "The Seven Habits of Highly Effective Teens" by Sean Covey. We began acknowledging students. Every Friday, anyone who had received a "Student of the Week" award was called out of the bleachers and given an award right then and there. That was intentional because traditional education isn't the coolest thing you can do in most inner cities, similar to Newark. I needed the masses to know that there were children who they thought weren't getting good grades that were doing great work. Teachers were acknowledging the roughest students, and were shocked and would say, "Whoa! Did he get a good grade? Is he getting a B? And I would pump it up: "Applaud them! Give it up!" We had to show that we would celebrate success. That was a structure we had changed that was transformational. We had a young man who was an average student. He had dropped out and began attending an alternative school. Finally, he came back to Shabazz, and he was trying to do right. The cool thing about the acknowledgment program wasn't that you just had to be passing. If you showed improvement, you would get an award. Three teachers recommended this young man for "Student of the Week" for his improved behavior. Here was a student who got seen as a horrible student, and he got acknowledged three times in one week. For him, it was game-changing. He put those awards in his book bag. He gave them to his mother, who was a teacher's aide at the school. It changed his trajectory, and I saw a change in his attitude and his respect for the school building. To him, it felt like, "I'm being recognized here, and not for bad things."

With a team entirely focused on climate and culture, student achievement and support services school became a safe place to be. We now had many things moving in the right direction that supports the mindset shift.

12 LEVER 3 INSTRUCTION

INSTRUCTION

How do we attack instruction powerfully? How do we ensure that there's going to be student achievement in Year One? To answer those questions it required a focus of not one administrator on the team, but a group of administrators hired to focus solely on improving teacher quality and student success in the classroom. Every instructional administrator was relieved of cafe duty, parent conferences, and disciplinary referrals. They were not responsible for doing any of that stuff. They were only responsible for going into classrooms on a regular basis, and determining what the deficiencies of the teachers were, and creating professional development around what teachers needed to be successful.

I wanted to ensure that students saw similar concepts in different classrooms. Thus, we identified subjects that shared curriculum standards and build on things that they were learning in other courses. For instance, we gave the entire freshman class algebra-based physics, and they also had algebra for double the time, which was more than any on grade level student. We also merged some of the language arts standards into history. We took writing and reading standards from language arts and applied them in Art courses and music courses. Language arts were the focus. We began to see progress because students started to master content that showed up in multiple classes throughout their day.

One of the things about instruction that can go wrong is that you can allow teachers to have the freedom to pick and choose what they think the students need versus what the state requires. I recall a teacher prepping 11th-grade students, who were special needs, using multiplication facts. That was not the best use of time; we could teach the students at this level how to use a calculator. It would be more of a tool than a crutch and move them along in the process of mastering some Algebra II standards. As a principal, when you're choosing the curriculum, it's crucial that you have teacher buy in to support the choices that you're making. Also, when the district is determining curriculum and superimposing it on teachers, it's imperative that they form a committee of administrators and classroom teachers to vet the curriculum before placing it in front of students, or it can fail miserably. For example, Newark was fed up with the traditional math curriculum, and went super-innovative, so innovative that the book chosen came with the resources needed to implement every lesson. This curriculum had students measuring how many calories got burned from a Frito chip. Teachings required Bunsen burners, beakers, lighters, and video. There were some of the most innovative things you could imagine happening in a classroom. But teachers weren't part of the selection process. The district spent $2 million to fill every class with this curriculum and teachers hated it. They didn't want to embrace it, and they struggled to implement some of the lessons because the training that was required forced them to take weekend classes. Even though they got paid for these courses, some teachers just didn't want to give up their weekends to receive that information. What I learned from the school district is, not only is it vital to inform teachers on what's going to be selected or has the potential to be chosen, but to gain their buy-in. Once you get buy-in from one teacher, you can get five, and from five you reach 10, and from 10 you can get 30 to 40 and potentially the whole building. The growth starts because a teacher has found it user-friendly and they're willing to explore more of the curriculum.

Initially, it was an easy fix. All we needed to do was implement the curriculum that the district selected. Because the school was so out of control, it was important just to have the students spend more time in the classroom on task. Solely by getting them into this place, working with teachers to professionally develop them on engaging students and using the curriculum that we already had, got us to 61 percent of language art proficiency. But now two years into the game we're up to 69 percent, and we're asking ourselves what's next. I began my doctorate studies at that time, and I learned about the eight-year study. It focused on a group of students who were allowed to enter college without completing the traditional processes to be accepted and a group of students who were required to get admitted the conventional way. Those students in the non-traditional acceptance process were allowed freedom in a way in which curriculum was taught to them. What the researchers found at the end of the study was that the students who had the privilege to receive curriculum in multiple subject areas in various ways without restriction outperformed the traditional cohort in college graduation, creating the indication that high school success was not a predictor on how students perform in college. The study allowed me to understand there are multiple ways you can expose children to the same standards in different courses in a very strategic way.

The Common Core national standards promoted this concept, but we didn't understand what they meant when they referred to literacy across the curriculum. Teachers were grappling with that idea, "So you're saying I should be doing English inside of math?" and that's not really what we were saying. We were saying that there is a literacy component of math that you should be able to master because there is a math language that existed. I began to look at how history and language arts attack the same standards for English Language Arts (ELA). We found that we could take a non-fiction document and begin to apply common core language arts standards. For example, Dr. Martin Luther King's Birmingham Address. If we started to dissect it, annotating as we go along and pulling factual evidence to support arguments, we could fully comprehend the meaning of each word and why he wrote them in such a way. When students see that they can think deeper, into why people make specific statements and use particular words, it's tremendous, and now the students are getting this kind of instruction double time. We're talking about 80 minutes of language arts. We're talking about an additional 80 minutes of history. It increases their ability to master language arts standards.

Another thing we were proud of was that we taught the sciences in a non-traditional sequence. The way that most high schools structure science is not necessarily the correct way. Traditionally the student would take biology, then chemistry, then physics would be the more challenging subject. What we find is that physics is very algebra-based. According to the National Science Foundation (NSF) and many other public policy groups, "placing physics first exposes more students to the discipline that provides the foundation for understanding engineering concepts and provides real-world connections to mathematical concepts. There is an organization I was able to partner with, called the Progressive Science Initiative, which created the curriculum that explicitly identified the overlap and how to teach it effectively. So every student who attended Shabazz High School as a freshman, whether special needs or regular education would need to take physics. They would participate in algebra-based physics and Algebra I, thereby doubling the amount of seat time they were having on the subject. Traditionally, a yearlong algebra class is 40 minutes, right? Well, what if we had a traditional algebra class go for 80 minutes all year long? That seat time is equivalent to more than two years of education if you were moving through a regular math class for five credits. Also, I paired history and language arts to add to the amount of focus on specific standards around. Aligning the curriculums increased student mastery of standards. The traditional structures existed we just had to rethink ways in which to get students to spend more time on them without it being obvious. Now they're doing math without realizing it. They're solving equations in physics. Now they're doing close reads on informational text in history, art, and health courses. It helped recover the deficiencies of the students who were entering the building. I am talking about students coming in on third-grade, fourth-grade ability levels in math now participating in a physics course as well as Algebra I classes and being able to get past the benchmark assessments we were given at that grade level. It happened because of our very intentional focus on the alliance of subject areas.

We Beta-tested many of these concepts before rolling it out building-wide. We had a competent teacher. Mrs. Bennett was her name. I remember saying, "Here's the catch. I want you to go get physics-certified." She replied that she was a math teacher. Why get physics-certified? "I'm no good in that," she said. "I do math!" So I told her that the New Jersey Center for Teaching and Learning (CTL) is pushing a new initiative called Progressive Science Initiative (PSI). They were willing to pay for teachers to take graduate courses as well as train them to implement PSI to students. In exchange, we would need her to teach one of the physics course during the school day. She agreed. The program gave clickers for the teachers through which they could create an interactive classroom, provide immediate data and feedback to students. The clickers raised the level of checking for understanding and mastery in classes. When other teachers visited the classroom, they began wanting to implement the process in their classroom as well. I even had a Spanish teacher ask if she could take the physics program because she, too, was interested in becoming certified.

Immersion in science and math was immense, especially for a teacher named Patrick Murray, who was a computer engineer who had retired from his private practice in which he had a ton of success, to become a math teacher. Within three years under me, he became my calculus teacher. That was huge. He was teaching Algebra I and worked hard to become a calculus teacher. With that, he brought a resource. We were prepping the students for physics and Algebra, and he was excited because he understood that we would have sophomores taking Advanced Placement physics and

Chemistry at the same time. He wrote the AP curriculum for the honors program to prepare the students for what came. In the midst of that, he wrote a grant with Dr. Steen, a research scientist at the University of Tennessee who got awarded a grant to work with high school students to conduct enzyme research. Mr. Murray took those children in partnership with the Poconos Environmental Education Center (PEEC) and had 15 students go to the Pocono Mountains and do enzyme studies on swamp water. It birthed a group of students from Newark, NJ, who now understood what it meant to be a research scientist. The program had Skype lessons inside of labs at Tennessee. From our understanding, swamp water is supposed to rid itself of this specific type of enzyme. When the students were testing the water, that wasn't the case. They found that it retained the enzyme that wasn't supposed to be there, which meant that something was happening to create the phenomenon. Our students discovered that while they were doing the research! It was a fantastic thing to see inner-city students who'd never been in the wilderness, with a scientist from one of the top universities in the country, solving rigorous equations to identify what's happening in various habitats.

We had reached a place where the students got exposed to new experiences and challenged in the classroom at all levels. By year three, all of the freshmen in the school were taking physics. I remember receiving a call from the creator of the program, Robert Goodman. He called and said he has a Senator from Utah, the Vice President of the New Jersey Education Association (NJEA) and ambassadors from Gambia Africa who would like to visit Shabazz High School to witness how the children are engaging with the PSI program. I'll never forget the day. We arrived early. I put together a schedule. They picked us up in a bus. The guest went in and out of classrooms, and they expressed how polite the children were, how it amazed them that children of that age could do physics problems at that level when Masters-educated adults couldn't solve them. All I could say was this is happening at Shabazz High School, a place where the students are the most at-risk by standardized test measures and also not necessarily viewed as the most successful. However the students were doing rigorous work, and people in positions of power were singing their praises. Utah's "Desert News" published an article written by US Senator Robert Bennett, who recently was on the visit at Shabazz high school. The Senator said "I took physics in both high school and college, and I didn't understand a word she was saying" yet "every student had the correct answer, showing that all understood." After the visit, "Gambian Ministry of Basic and Secondary education in collaboration with the New Jersey for Teaching and Learning began training 48 teachers in Progressive Science Initiative and Progressive Mathematics Initiative."

Robert is brilliant. When you meet him you know, he's a smart man and knows his stuff. Robert especially knows his physics. But he doesn't give you much about who he is. Robert was a physics teacher in Bergen

County Technical Schools. He decided that there was a massive issue in physics and that there needed to be more physics teachers within our schools to increase the number of students going into the field. Robert created a program to streamline certifying physics teachers. The program works; he got a ton of funding, there are tons of teachers around the state and now in other countries, who are embracing and implementing this concept.

13

LEVER 4
PROFESSIONAL
DEVELOPMENT

This lever is all about teacher quality. Building an organization by focusing on your students without making the same commitment to your staff will not succeed for long. Professional development (PD) is probably the most underrated lever in most schools. Many administrators do not plan to have professional development embedded into the school day. PD happens after school and does not connect with the entire process. Many educators view PD as something that occurs when students are off. It is imperative that we take PD seriously. Teachers must be scheduled into workshops and focus on a specific area of growth. Educators are not always present to the power of professional development. One of the things we take for granted is that educators know all about their field and that they have what it takes because they've earned a college degree. However, just because somebody has a Masters or a Doctorate, we must take into account that things change as students grow. Teachers must engage students differently. There was a time when there were no computers. Now the cell phone has taken over, and students are fully capable of texting 50 to 60 words per minute. How do we begin to prepare teachers for that climate to better engage their students? It was essential to focus on ways we engage students through the growth of teachers; they needed training on cutting-edge engagement strategies. Teachers needed to be as current as possible on innovative ways to engage students because they are evolving daily. Therefore, the teaching staff got required to develop and deliver rigorous lessons to our students.

We cannot underestimate the power of professional development and teachers getting together for the greater good of the process. It sounds great to have this time, but many leaders get the time, and it's very unstructured. Thus, leaving teachers to do what they want. One of the things that were extremely important for me was having alignment around PD so the administration could genuinely be able to deliver sufficient professional development. The months before school began we spent our time creating a professional development plan. It got derived from evaluation data we collected at the end of the previous school year. So based on the data, collectively, from every evaluation done in this school for a full year, as well as walkthrough data, we identified the weakest indicators regarding teacher practice, which told us where to focus at the start of the school year. At the time it was student engagement. From there we decided to identify a research-based text that's user-friendly that our teachers could study. That way we could build out a yearlong plan, or at least a half-year plan before we could reassess what the next steps were. We chose "Teach Like a Champion," which was 50 well-articulated engagement strategies that teachers could implement in the classroom. We understood that giving them the book would not suffice. We needed every teacher engaging with this text and could not allow some teachers to do it and some not to participate.

Administrators were required to create professional development modules that got delivered to their teachers based on specific concepts that we chose from "Teach Like a Champion." We would choose two to three strategies at a time, and every Wednesday and Thursday, teachers would receive professional development regarding the "Teach Like a Champion" engagement strategies. The philosophy was, if we select three strategies, teachers would be required to decide which strategy they want to focus on for the duration of the module and implement during delivery of their lessons. No matter what subject you were teaching, you could say, "My strategy for today is 'No Opt Out.'" "No Opt Out" is a practice, which encourages students to answer when they are unable or unwilling to participate. The strategy helped to mitigate any perception that educators were calling students out or picking on them, or "You're purposely choosing me because I'm not sure what's going on." The strategy was designed to inform the student that we're going to be doing "No Opt Out," which means that if I call on you, I expect you to respond. Your answer may be right, it may be wrong, either way, it's okay, but we need something to start the conversation for us to build on with the other student so we can get to the proper answer if the student did not have it. It was empowering for a student to know that we were functioning in the class this way, to prevent embarrassment if they didn't have the right answer. They would feel comfortable giving their thoughts, versus shutting down, being disrespectful or feeling as if, "Why are you talking to me about this thing that you know I don't know?" So I would go into the classroom and see if the teachers are doing this and give teachers feedback on how they were doing with implementation.

As you're reading this, you may be wondering, "where did they find the time to implement all of this?" We looked at the schedule and asked ourselves how can we carve out time for teachers to be together, to discuss disciplinary issues, planning, etc. How does math teachers meet with math teachers to plan and to look at data to see what's working in those classrooms? We found that there were common times where teachers had preparation periods and could meet. Also, because the administration built the plan before teachers arrived for the new year, we were able to reconfigure some of the master schedules to allow teachers of the same subject to meet for "Common Planning" on multiple days. Thus, all interdisciplinary planning time was held on Thursday and titled "Professional Learning Communities" (PLCs) and all departmental planning was titled "Common Planning Time" (CPT) and held on Tuesdays of each week. Teachers were not required to meet together on the other days. The interdisciplinary professional development allowed us to create unique partnerships such as the culinary arts teacher designing lessons with a math teacher. We understood that we needed to focus on common core curriculum standards and how to engage students rigorously. The subject areas taught became less and less relevant. Thus, if we showed an art teacher, a music teacher, a history teacher, an english teacher, a math teacher and a science teacher five research-based engagement strategies, then it wouldn't matter what subject they were teaching. They could all go into a classroom and use the think-pair-share strategy.

In the think-pair-share strategy, teachers disseminate information to students groups, and students would work together to develop a response to the questions asked. Then each group would share with the class while the teacher facilitated the process. That's one strategy that crosses multiple disciplines. Another approach that got utilized, one that I loved, I called The Carousel. No matter what subject you were in, it was something that would engage children. Sometimes teachers believe that fun activity equal engagement. Like counting pieces of cereal, or putting things in paper bags or measuring things or bouncing balls. Those are activities that can exist only in some disciplines.

In The Carousel, if I taught math, and I was teaching equations, I would post six pieces of chart paper around my classroom, create six groups, and have them solve equations on the board. They would have three minutes to answer it and then rotate to the next problem. As one group switches to the following chart paper, the students are responsible for analyzing the previous group's steps for solving the problem. In the end, we'll have six teams responding to six different equations and evaluating another group's work six times.

As a new principal with a new administrative team, we could not have accomplished all of what has been outlined above by our selves. I had support from an astounding partner that was able to provide us with the tools we needed for success as well as fill in the gaps created from our inexperience. I was fortunate enough to work with Seton Hall University in my first year as a principal. Sometimes consultants come in, do an excellent job or not, nonetheless they do not stay long because schools can no longer afford them. I refused to let that happen. My requirement for Seton Hall was to teach the administrators how to create and conduct professional development for their teachers. The Seton Hall representatives were not allowed to present to teachers. They were only allowed to meet with and help coach the administration through the process of creation and delivery and then monitor their implementation. It is difficult to sustain a six-figure PD bill year after year; especially when budget cuts are coming down the pike like you wouldn't believe. It was essential that our administrative team develop this skillset because educating adults is different than teaching students. Adults learn, pushback, and engage differently. Therefore, don't think that you're going to go in and talk to a bunch of teachers and they're going to retain all of the information presented and deliver it correctly. No! Teachers want to participate too. They want to do think-pair-shares as participants. They want to create. They want to share ideas. They want to experience PD the way students experience lessons.

14

LEVER 5
MONITORING

MONITORING

The last and most important lever is monitoring. One can talk about having a unique instructional program, or about structures, or about professional development. However, you have to inspect what you expect. We tried a ton of researched-based strategies and decided not to hope something worked. Collecting data on each approach chosen was imperative. Teachers needed to see the results of their efforts as well as have a clear understanding of what needed to be improved and why. Administrators had to be able to differentiate their professional development for the teachers they supervised. Our team would do 60 to 100 walkthroughs a week. On a bi-weekly basis, we would look at the data to figure out where our issues were with teacher performance and with student performance. The walkthroughs align with our teacher evaluation tool. The entire school district agreed that it defined what highly effective teaching looks like in the classroom.

Newark Public Schools Framework for Effective Teaching

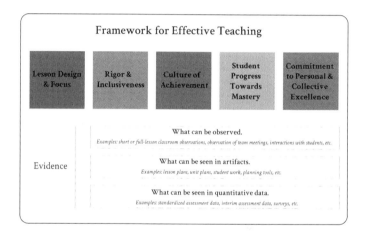

We reviewed walkthrough data twice a month and were able to compare progression over time.

Walkthrough Data Report - December 23, 2013

Administrator	Department	Tally	% of group
Administrator A	English & Social Studies	31	49.2%
Administrator B	Mathematics & Science	10	15.8%
Administrator C	World Language & CTE	10	15.8%
Administrator D	Health & PE	0	0%
All Administrators	Special Education	7	11.1%
Gemar Mills	All	5	7.9%
	Total	63	100%

You might be asking, "How do you do 60 to 100 walk-throughs in two weeks and have a ton of other things to do?" Remember, we restructured our administrative cabinet, which allowed administrators to take on the same amount of work rooted in one particular area such as instruction, climate, and culture, or support services. We had a group of administrators focused only on going into the classroom. They didn't deal with discipline; we had another group of people for that. Narrowing the focus of each administrator is how you get them to monitor the most critical components in a school.

We needed to know the things that were commonly showing up. The report I created is broken down into four competencies and 18 performance indicators. We spent most of our time focusing on competencies two and three because they were observable inside the classroom. In year one we noticed that our teachers uti-lized a lot of their instructional time providing direct instruction. Direct instruction created a significant level of student disengagement according to the data, behavioral issues, and forced us to place very close at-tention to teacher lesson plans. The monitoring pro-cess and the data we gleaned from it were incredibly compelling. It gave us a place to focus. Often, we as educators focus on things that *seem* to be the problem and hope that they work, whereas the data allows us to zero in on what our priority instructional focuses are. When we were going into a classroom, we noticed that teachers were talking too much and students were disconnected entirely and having behavior problems. Instead of focusing on strictly engagement and behavior management, we found that we needed to take a more in-depth look at lesson planning. Teachers were planning their lessons and delivering them as they designed them. As administrators, we were failing to take a closer look at the plans long before they even got into the classroom. The data shifted our focus from student engagement to lesson planning during the early months of the turnaround.

In that first quarter, we had to focus on getting teachers to understand the importance of three-part objectives and how to use them to refocus instruction. How to construct a three-part goal so that the condition, behavior, and measure existed in everyone posted on the board. Also, each teacher created a demonstration of learning, which was a task a student needed to complete before leaving the class on that day. These tasks allowed the teacher to determine if students had mastered the skill or the behavior of focus on that particular day. We spent time developing the right lesson plan tools for teachers to create these lessons successfully. We provided them with strategies and helped them design questions to get asked during a classroom lesson. We spent time on that before moving on to student engagement strategies and professional development. The lesson-planning phase was grueling. There was a lot of one-on-one and differentiating amongst the staff. All the teachers didn't need the same level of focus for us to roll out a full-on professional development plan solely on lesson planning and design. However, the process still required our administrators to have relentless focus, follow-up, and consistency with our teachers to improve their practice.

We conducted a group walkthrough once a month to ensure that our lens was normed, which strengthened administrators ability to ascertain the same under-

---

Administrative Walkthrough Guidelines

Preparation
- Principal prepares staff members for walkthrough.
- Principal identifies the focus for the walkthrough and the classrooms that will be visited.
- School improvement consultant determines each person's responsibility during the walkthrough for the following:
  - 1-Focus
  - 2-Three-Part Lesson Objective
  - 3-Preparation for Instruction (Instruction)
  - 4- Use of Data to Inform Instruction
  - 5- Student Engagement (Instruction)
  - 6- Effective Instruction/Student Communication
  - 7- Classroom Environment-Wall Walk
  - 8- Student Interviews
- One person will monitor the time.
- If possible, principal will have staff set the following items in key locations to facilitate walkthrough: student work products, lesson plans, recent assessments, and portfolios.

Walkthrough
Time: 8-10 minutes per classroom (person monitoring time will signal)

- Team members enter classroom together and do not speak to each other during their time in the classroom.
- Team members stand at back of classroom unless they have a specific assignment to talk to students or examine student work.
- At the end of agreed-upon time, all team members leave the classroom together.

Debriefing – Outside the classroom
Time: 5 minutes per classroom

- Team members make notes.
- Team members walk a short distance down the hall from the observed classroom.
- Speaking quietly, team members quickly share their observations regarding the last classroom visited.
- Team members proceed to next classroom.

Debriefing – Final
Time: 25 minutes

- Walkthrough team members assemble in agreed-upon meeting place.
- Each visitor reads over and reflects about his or her observations.
- Each visitor speaks about his or her observations. They provide specific evidence as well as attempt to present an overview of what they saw.
- Together, the members identify trends, areas of strength, and areas that need improvement.
- Drawing on their own experience and knowledge, the visitors make suggestions about themes to be addressed

standing of something when observed separately. The norming process was very intense; it took half a school day to complete this task.

On norming days the administration would do some pre-planning. I would have the scheduling vice-principal look at teachers who were available from first through the fourth period and group the administration team. What I mean by that is if there were four administrators on that given day we would pair them by twos. If it were six to nine administrators including school officials from central office, we would form groups of three. We would often invite district-level officials to participate in our norming process because we needed an unbiased eye to be sure we were seeing what we thought we were seeing and that our understanding of the evaluation tool was the same as administrators who assisted in creating the evaluation tool. We would send administration teams to various sections of the school building, intentionally placing a group of administrators on each floor. Sometimes we would leave out either the fourth floor or the gymnasium or the first or second. Ultimately we would get in my conference room, take a look at the schedule, decide on a time that we would return to the conference room, and head out for our group walkthroughs.

Our goal was to conduct as many walkthroughs as possible, as a group, within the first four periods of our school day. Teams would go in for 6 to 10 minutes, step outside the classroom to debrief immediately and each person would report out their portion of the walkthrough and have a scholarly discussion. We would have a dialogue about what we saw. Was our interpretation of the lesson the same or different? Was the administrator's understanding of the indicator correct? The group walkthrough process was great for discussion and made sure we were all on the same page. It exposed some of our administrators' weaknesses with the evaluation tool, which was essential to improving their depth of knowledge and use of the tool. The administrators' familiarity with the evaluation tool was crucial because they were going into a classroom to determine if a teacher was highly effective or ineffective or partially effective. From there we would come back to our meeting space. We would identify what the strengths and weaknesses were from our observations. Each group was required to complete a tally sheet that would allow us to see on average how teachers were performing. Then we would report out, and we would aggregate all our findings. What we'd find was that there were similarities even though we were in various parts of the school building with different administrators observing different teachers. We would take that information and share the findings with the entire staff, and create next steps for professional development to come. As a principal it allowed me to see where I needed to go with my administrative team, how I needed to develop them professionally to make them stronger leaders for teachers as we moved forward in this monitoring process.

I recall discovering that we had an issue with student engagement according to the data. We started off well, and then we had a dip in mid-March. The data helped us find out why. What's happening here? We instituted focus areas for student interviews. We asked them what they were learning, why they were learning it, and to whom could they go to get help? We watched from March to June that students began to understand, after we told them over and over, that they go to a student first before asking a teacher.

To keep our finger on the pulse of student achievement, we conducted monthly benchmark assessments. It would show how many students were below, above or need intervention, or on the watch for intervention. We did the same thing with math. In 2010, our language arts scores were 44%. A year later they inched up to 46%. My first year as principal, 2011-12, we went to 60%, a 14% gain. In math, Shabazz students tested at 21.3% in 2010. My first year as principal, in one school year, we rose 8.1%. The structures we created supported all the school's growth.

Professional Development monitoring was equally important as any other monitoring system we decided to implement within the school. When building this system, I wanted to be sure of two things. One, a teacher walked away satisfied with the training they received and two how many hours of professional development did each teacher accumulate each quarter.

We created collaborative planning time and grade level communities. Each community had a leader that focused on the priorities set forth by him or her in conjunction with the administrator. Our structure supported that. As we built the master schedule, we ensured that math teachers had the same preparation period two days a week. The same was true for English teachers and all other teacher groups. The structures helped us pull together combinations of teachers to have joint planning time. Teachers were able to say, "You teach algebra, I teach algebra. Let's bring sample work; let's see how students are performing on specific things. If they are not making progress, what are your best practices? What can we learn from each other?

Monitoring discipline is essential. No different than our approach monitoring instruction, we did not want to guess why students were getting into trouble. We decided to identify a system that could help us be as consistent as possible, as well as monitor data no different than what we would monitor anything else. The On Course system assisted us with this as well. It let us aggregate teacher electronic disciplinary infraction forms. Often the process would lead to a parent conference. These conferences would force teachers to have interactions with parents because the parents had to come in for the student to return to school. There were things as small as a student disrespecting a teacher by cursing at them, or things as big as a student attempting to assault a teacher. No matter how big or small it was, we wanted to ensure that parents were coming into the school and dealing with whatever inconsistencies the students had. It was imperative that parents, teachers, and administrators could work together toward getting any student to increased academic success. We didn't want to allow it to fall by the wayside because a parent had to go to work. That wasn't acceptable.

When we talk about monitoring, we built a fantastic system because it allowed us to pinpoint where the issues were, like which grade levels were having the most problems, and what were the recurring infractions. One fight can sometimes be so big that no one ever forgets it, and the thinking becomes that fighting is the problem, so we need to keep children from fighting. But we found that seniors and juniors got in trouble a lot less than first-year students and sophomores. It seemed that the freshmen were more active in getting in trouble than any other group. It made sense because they were immature. Also, we discovered the most frequent type of infraction. The freshman and sophomores were very juvenile, so they were continually getting in trouble for disrespecting the teacher, for not doing what the teacher asked, talking in class. We needed to get out in front of that. One of the things we were able to do was identify supports outside the school and develop our supports inside the schoolhouse. Our goal was to educate the children on how to interact with one another, with adults, and the can and can not at Shabazz High School. These were all things that allowed us to get out in front of low student behavior, which had become the standard. The administrative team and staff were giving students the knowledge to make the decisions that they needed to make before they even got in trouble. It was also easier to deal with it because if a student got in trouble over something we had already explained was unacceptable, there wasn't an argument from the parent, and there wasn't an argument from the student. We issued the reprimand, and then the student went back to class. Everyone was on the same page. Consistency was paramount in mitigating student misbehavior in classrooms. The reports provided charts of which grades had the most infractions, and which grade levels' violations were most common. Was it fighting? Was it disrespect to teachers? The behavioral data collection helped us take pro-active approaches to eliminating disrespect to staff members. We had to role-play for the freshmen because they could not articulate a misunderstanding without hitting each other. We learned that through data. We determined which class was the most aggressive, and why. We discovered it by monitoring the systems we put in place. Men lie, women lie, but numbers do not.

15 GOING FORWARD

GOING FORWARD

I'm no longer at Shabazz, having moved on to an organization called The Future Project, dedicated to helping our youth become "Possibility Thinkers" through
a methodology that allows them to dream and distill
their passion in life and the power that come from it to
trail blaze their path to success. Is my work at Shabazz
finished? Yes and no. On the one hand, the progress
is undeniable. Thousands of students graduated and
went on to four-year universities. On the other, turnarounds are seldom finished or permanent. They are
more of a process than an event. In life, if you're not
moving forward, you're likely sliding backward. But
the levers work. Shabazz is proof. No longer can stu-

dents boast to state monitors that they run the school. Pulling alarms is no longer the norm.

Graduation Day is a triumph not only for Shabazz and its students and teachers but for anyone who wants to believe that change is possible. Turnarounds are possible everywhere, whether in people or institutions. It's there if you want it.

Students showed us signs that things were working, Shabazz was undergoing a shift in culture. What may best illustrate it was our valedictorian, Elmy Antonio. He was part of the freshman class we welcomed in my first year as principal. He was a small kid, and not very outgoing. But Elmy was relentless at getting things done inside the classroom. Our teachers took a liking to him quickly. He was not the kind of student you would look at and immediately project to be our valedictorian. But on his first report card, he received straight A's. He kept getting straight A's for his entire freshman year, and that's not necessarily the norm for young minority males.

In his sophomore year, Elmy pursued an interest in baseball while maintaining his excellence in the classroom. He grew a little bigger, got a little cooler, got more friends. Elmy's attributes were essential to our school culture because we had a young man who was getting it done both in and out of the classroom, and he became an influence on others. To the naked eye, you would never know that Elmy had the highest GPA in the school. He graduated from high school with an above average GPA.

It was a fantastic story to share with others.

It was quite a thing to watch how much resilience he had and continued to exhibit for four straight years no matter what the pressures were from his peers. Elmy always kept his eyes on the prize and did everything his mom asked him. Most important, Elmy motivated other young men who didn't think education was the coolest thing.

Remember the phrases "By any means necessary" and "failure is not an option?" They apply not only to the work we did but also to myself. Many of us coast through life without ambition. We work jobs we do not like until the day we die. That's the mindset of the majority of Americans, and that simply would not work for someone in the "By any means necessary" category. If you are accepting of what is and do not seek to change it, then you will struggle to be a great leader. You MUST change before you can turn around any organization and lead others. The confinement of your thoughts won't allow you to take the necessary risk because your fixating on what exists and not the possibility that the uncertainty can generate an abundance of success. Once you have the mindset that change is not only necessary but also possible, it is important to find others who have a similar mindset and are willing to follow a strong leader. Your team is one of the most valuable assets of your organization, but putting that team together can be a tiring process. I intentionally seek to work with people who possess a fervent ability to persevere, which is undoubtedly beneficial to the process in which I'm involved.

Sometimes you will be at a loss about who these people will be or how you will identify their skillsets to place them on your team. However, you must trust the process and have faith that your plan will work. I have always felt my work in education was bigger than me. I felt like the universe, or a higher power continues to conspire to do this higher good for my passion and purpose in the world. It's something I believe in, and I think that God puts the right people in front of us and we can accomplish some amazing things that could not get fulfilled without these relationships. I didn't create PSI. I just knew that it was appropriate for children. They needed it to strengthen their ability in Algebra because it is the most failed subject in America.

One must believe in his or her students and staff members. Your belief in them gives them the drive needed to "show up" whenever possible. My message to my team was, "You have the ability, and you want this? Yes! Then I am going to create the environment in which everyone feels comfortable being educated, educating, and excited about coming to school each day. Those students who were once angry, disengaged, and out of control were now happy to get to class, be respectful, and engaged in lessons. Those teachers who were once uninspired, disconnected, and accepting of the status quo were now happy to report to work, be coached, and teach amazing lessons.

As you go through life and try to figure out what your

purpose is, you are steadily doing a lot of things that you may not be passionate about, not knowing if there's a purpose in those experiences. You don't necessarily know if it's right for you. Thus you go through hurt and pain to learn. Through this process, you discover your passion and purpose in life. At one point, I had a shallow intention. It was all about money. I wanted a lot of it. When I finally accepted that I needed to have a purpose, which I wouldn't give up on something I truly believed in, something I was passionate about, money began to follow me. I didn't wish for it anymore. I had to start turning it down because I was taking on so much that I couldn't keep up with what people were offering. It had nothing to do with a scheme or a strategy. It had to do with putting my heart and my energy all into the greater good of another human being.

I realize that the things I went through with my mother, learning from her and her struggle, things that I went through as a child in the projects, experiencing stuff that I never thought I should be experiencing, was prepping me for a specific outcome. It all had to do with children like me with some of the most troubling backgrounds who face the similar obstacles. Helping them navigate that terrain was possible only because I had lived it. Thinking that I was going be an athlete or a real estate broker and watching those things come and go prepared me for this education. No matter what was happening in my life education found me. In high school, I remembered passing my standardized test the first time around and got an opportunity to tutor eighth-grade students at one of the middle-schools in Paterson. I remember substitute teachings at the age of 19 years old and enjoying every minute of the experience. I remember becoming an Assistant Director at the Boys and Girls club and tutoring students in Math and Science. All of these occurrences were pushing me in that direction, despite me running from my purpose in life. Once I embraced it, within five years of my educational career, I was a high school principal.

If your school is new, then success is about locating individuals that possess resilience, grit, learn from others, and can work well with others. The interviewing process will be a vital piece to ensure that they understand your goals and methods to reach success. If you are taking over the reins of an established school, then you need to assess your staff and be prepared to make changes seriously. Your faculty is integral, but once your people are in place, then it's time to focus on the reason you are all there, the students. You may think that teaching is about applying the knowledge of a subject matter and transferring that knowledge to your students. That's not accurate, though. The fact is, education is more about translation than anything else. Sure you may all speak English, but that's not the language barrier I am referencing. You must learn body language, shifts in behaviors, and how to converse with a students heart before talking to their brain.

You cannot teach the same way for inner-city youth as you do for students within suburban townships. There is a cultural roadblock that can leave one side in the dark while the other group understands the subject without hindrance. Empathy and culture sensitivity is hugely significant.

Success comes from taking the best from both past and the present. There's no need to throw everything away and do something different. We need to embrace the things that have worked, that have shown promise, which excite teachers. We need to think about more innovative ways to engage students in that process. The curriculum does not need to be different. But maybe the way a teacher prepares a lesson for that curriculum needs to change. When we do professional development, we should focus more on the person who's delivering the exercise than on throwing out the actual lesson and replacing it with something that's less familiar to the person who must teach it. That can be more of a detriment than a mechanism to maximize student achievement.

Life is a feeling process. Sometimes you have to utilize your intuition to decide what you're going to do next. I'm thankful I went with my gut on a lot of what I thought would work for children despite watching principal after principal try and fail, and not acknowledging my ability.

There wasn't a well-thought-out plan that I had when I began. I just had this belief that if I did it my way it would work. I feel that anyone who is reading this book has the one-up on me because you have the theory and the practice. Now you have the opportunity to do even grander and more significant things for more students throughout our country. I think it is the time that we embrace this as a challenge and seek to have massive turnarounds in a short period that will yield results so America can be known for its excellent educational system once again.

WORKS CITED

Bollman, Lee G. and Deal, Terrence E. Reframing Organizations: Artistry, Choice, and Leadership. San Francisco: John Wiley & Sons, 2013.

Covey, Sean. The 7 Habits of Highly Successful Teens. New York: Touchstone, 1998.

Dweck, Carol S., Ph.D. Mindset: The New Psychology of Success. New York: Random House, 2007. Print.

Fullan, Michael, Leading in a Culture of Change. San Francisco: John Wiley & Sons, 2004.

Fullan, Michael, The Six Secrets of Change. San Francisco: John Wiley & Sons, 2008.

Limov, Doug and Atkins, Norman, Teach Like a Champion: 49 Techniques That Put Students on the Path to College. San Francisco: John Wiley & Sons, April 2010.

Mathematics, Science Teachers Begin 10-Day Training. Daily Observer forward with The Gambia. https://njctl-media.s3.amazonaws.com/uploads/public-Mathematics-science-teachers-begin-10-day-training-Daily-Observer.pdf

NPS Framework for Effective Teacher, Newark Public Schools, December 19, 2016. http://www.nps.k12.nj.us/evaluation-resources/teacher-evaluations/

Physics First, American Association of Physics Teachers. Pamphlet https://www.aapt.org/Resources/upload/PHYS_first.pdf

Roy, M. Saving Shabazz. Star-Ledger article and documentary. NJ.com. April 24, 2013 http://www.nj.com/hssports/blog/football/index.ssf/2013/04/starledger_documentary_saving_shabazz_the_long-shot_battle_to_transform_a_failing_school.html

School-to-Prison Pipeline (n.d.), ACLU Website https://www.aclu.org/feature/school-prison-pipeline

Tanner, Daniel and Tanner, Laurel N. Curriculum Development: Theory into Practice. New York: Macmillan, 1980.

Technology can change education, Bennett, Robert. Deseret News, April 23, 2012. http://www.deseretnews.com/article/765570717/Technology-can-change- education.html

The History of Violence as a Public Health Issue. Center of Disease Control Website http://www.cdc.gov/violenceprevention/pdf/history_violence-a.pdf
    Reprinted from: Dahlberg LL, Mercy JA. AMA Virtual Mentor, February 2009. Volume 11, No. 2: pp. 167-172.

Tough, Paul. How Children Succeed: Grit, Curiosity, and Hidden Power of Character. Boston, New York: Houghton, Mifflin, Harcourt, 2012.